# Eddie Waring

# ON RUGBY LEAGUE

*Above:* Widnes players,
Cunningham, Gregory, Gorley and
Prescott celebrate their victory over Hull
Kingston Rovers in the 1981 Cup Final.

*Below:* Saint Helens versus Hull Kingston
Rovers in the 1981 semi-final

# Eddie Waring

## ON
## RUGBY LEAGUE

Frederick Muller Limited
London

First published in Great Britain 1981 by Frederick Muller Limited,
London NW2 6LE

Waring, Eddie
    Eddie Waring on Rugby League.
    1.  Rugby football – History
    1.Title
    796.3330904        GV944.85

    ISBN 0-584-10358-1

Phototypeset by Input Typesetting Ltd, London SW19 8DR
Printed in Great Britain by Butler and Tanner Ltd., Frome and
London

# CONTENTS

# INTRODUCTION

Thirteen, unlucky for some they say but not for Rugby League, the thirteen a-side version of the oval ball game.

Born in 1895 when 20 clubs broke away from the Rugby Union to form the Northern Union the game was given only a few years to live. It survived a shaky start and has since experienced plenty of high and low points until today it is established as a major part of the British sporting scene.

The rift with the Rugby Union occurred largely because some strong Northern clubs insisted on recompensing their players for loss of earnings as a result of taking part in Rugby Football. The Northern teams were drawn chiefly from the working classes amongst whom the roots of Rugby League were proudly nurtured. These days, however, those who play and support the game are found in all walks of life and from many different backgrounds.

There are some thirty professional clubs located in the north of England which operate on a part-time basis. The bye-laws forbid a player to make a living solely from the game and at the professional level the players are paid only when they play and are paid well, by the games' relatively modest standards, only when they win.

Many people outside the traditional Rugby League areas labour under the misconception that the game is entirely professional. Nothing could be further from the truth! Each weekend tens of thousands of players enjoy the sport purely for the love of the game in matches in the amateur leagues and in the universities, colleges and schools. Indeed, thanks to the splendid work of the British Amateur Rugby League Association founded in

Eddie Waring leading the singing

1973, Rugby League is one of Britain's fastest growing amateur sports.

Abroad the game is strongest in Australia, particularly in Sydney, which boasts the most prosperous clubs in the Rugby League world. New Zealand, France and most recently Papua New Guinea, have also taken firmly to the game. Rugby League's traditional skill, speed and toughness would seem to make it a "natural" for the American sporting scene and vigorous efforts are underway to establish the game in the U.S.A.

Rugby League has been a major television sport for over 25 years. It is no exaggeration to say that the game has become a national sport through the medium of T.V. with millions of people enjoying the live televising of matches in B.B.C.'s Grandstand most Saturdays throughout the winter as well as the very popular floodlit tournament on B.B.C. 2. The success of the game of T.V. has made it very attractive to sponsors of sport today with the professional teams competing for prize money totalling well over £250,000 per season in the various sponsored competitions – not bad for what was once a cinderella sport of proud but humble origins!

Without doubt, the greatest single day in Rugby League's calendar is the Challenge Cup Final at Wembley early each May. Currently sponsored by State Express, the Challenge Cup Competition first took place in 1897, Batley, "the gallant youths" being the first winners. For over 80 years the Challenge Cup has consistently produced moments of high drama and countless deeds of derring-do. Each time I take up the T.V. commentary position near the top of the South stand at the famous Empire Stadium my thoughts return to 1929 when Dewsbury took on Wigan in the first ever Challenge Cup Final at Wembley. The immortal Jim Sullivan, a magnificent full back, led Wigan, a team of many talents, against Dewsbury, a side of home grown footballers. It is said that Dewsbury were told to play open football in order to make a good impression on the London public but this was not Dewsbury's normal style. They lost and received £3.00 per man along with their losers' medals, which the players characteristically considered to be beyond price. Skill, courage, drama, the brotherhood of celebrated stars and grass-roots heroes – these are the ingredients which make Rugby League the greatest game of all for me and many thousands of folk who, like me, thrill to its red-blooded exponents and love its no-nonsense style.

*Eddie Waring*

*June 1981*

# 1

# A BRIEF HISTORY OF THE GAME OF RUGBY LEAGUE

The game we now know as Rugby League was born on Thursday 29th August, 1895. Appropriately enough its cradle was a solid four square Victorian edifice, the George Hotel, in the centre of Huddersfield. The birth pangs had been long and painful, for the game resulted from one of the greatest rows in British sporting history. It is never easy to trace the roots of a major squabble. Frequently, "the row is not what the row is all about", as they say in Yorkshire. Essentially, however, it was a row between North and South, between the representatives of the working classes and the leisured classes, between attitudes which differed sharply about the emphasis to be placed on the recreational and competitive elements in sport. The rugby players in the close-knit northern communities were always aware of the existence of successful, well-organised, fully professional soccer clubs in the same towns where they themselves were actually losing money in order to play their chosen sport.

In the 1890s the average wage of a miner or a mill worker was 26/- for a 5½ day working week based on lengthy shifts. Travelling to play in a rugby match often meant losing a shift and consequent financial hardship for the predominantly working class members of the northern teams. On the other hand, the southern players, drawn largely from university and public school backgrounds, could comfortably withstand the cost of playing. For some years it was alleged that northern clubs were in the practice of making "broken time" payments to their players, i.e. recompense for loss of earnings as a result of playing rugby. This and allied changes were the subject of a long-standing controversy within the Rugby Union.

Matters came to a head at the Annual General Meeting of the Rugby Football Union held in London on September 20th, 1893, in an attempt to regularise the situation so that, "things now done stealthily could be done in the light of day." Mr J. A. Miller, President of the Yorkshire Rugby Football Union, proposed that it should be permissible for players to be compensated for bona-fide loss of time. The secretary of the Rugby Union, Rowland Hill, moved an amendment declining to sanction broken-time payments because the principle was, "contrary to the true interest of the game and its spirit" Hill's amendment was carried by two-hundred and eighty-two votes to one-hundred and thirty-six, though one-hundred and twenty votes cast in favour were proxies amassed before the meeting. The northern clubs were by no means discouraged and since during the next two years the Rugby Union passed even more stringent rules against broken-time payments the inevitable break between the northern clubs and the London headquarters became only a matter of time.

On August 29th, 1895, twenty-one clubs from Yorkshire and Lancashire attended a special meeting at Huddersfield. Twenty clubs voted to break away and form a new organisation to be called the Northern Rugby Football Union. Of the clubs at this historic meeting, only Dewsbury voted against the formation of the Northern Union. The founder members were:

In Yorkshire – Batley, Bradford, Brighouse Rangers, Halifax, Huddersfield, Hull, Hunslet, Leeds, Liversedge, Manningham and Wakefield Trinity.

In Lancashire – Broughton Rangers, Leigh, Oldham, Rochdale, St Helens, Tyldesley, Warrington, Wigan and Widnes.

The Cheshire clubs Runcorn and Stockport, joined the rebels in time to start the inaugural season. It was formally agreed that "the idea of the break-away was that to live honestly under the proposed new rules of the English Rugby Union was a moral impossibility and much as we may regret the severance from the parent body the bulk of the far-seeing football enthusiasts are unanimous in their opinion that the time has come to "kick" against the ridiculous rules and demands of the "Old Lady" at Conduit Vale, ie. the Rugby Union at its London Headquarters.

Though the broken-time issue had been the chief motivating factor in its foundation, initially the Northern Union took a hard line against open professionalism. A ceiling of 6/- per day was fixed to recompense players for genuine loss of earnings, all players had to have full-time employment outside Rugby Football and heavy fines and suspensions were imposed on offenders. Open professionalism was eventually recognised in 1898 but players still had to be otherwise employed in "legitimate" jobs. Bookies runner, billiard-hall marker, and barman did not count! Today's professional rugby players still operate on a part-time basis. They must be employed outside football; they are paid only when they play and are paid well only when they win.

The administrators of the Northern Union quickly realised that if players were to be paid then more spectators would have to be attracted and the turnstiles kept clicking. The traditional Rugby Union game was in the main a close marking affair, short on spectacle and therefore lacking crowd appeal. In the first two seasons of its existence the Northern Union stuck to traditional rules involving line outs and the eight-man scrummage. In 1897, however, the gap between the two Unions was widened immeasureably when the Northern Union abolished the line out and tested various methods of recommencing play from touch. Scoring values were also amended. A try was deemed to be worth 3 points and any type of goal two points. There followed a decade or so of amazing activity which established beyond recall the essentials of the Rugby League game we know today as a tough, fast, spectacular, competitive sport played on a world-wide scale.

To northern folk, in those days as now, competition was the essence of any sporting encounter. From its inception the Northern Union operated on a competitive basis encompassing two major leagues – the Lancashire Senior Competition and the Yorkshire Senior Competition. In only its second season the new body, with a keen eye on the Football Association's most profitable money spinner, introduced a knock-out competition, the Northern Union Challenge Cup open to all member clubs. The first final on May 1st, 1897, drew 13,490 spectators paying £624 pounds to see Batley beat St. Helens by 10 points to 3 at the Leeds club's fine new stadium, Headingley. Stirring inter-county clashes in the Challenge Cup soon brought a demand for establishing a super-league involving the cream of the clubs from the Senior Competitions. Representatives of twelve of the strongest clubs meeting at Huddersfield in May 1901 drew up a resolution that a Northern Rugby League should be formed, consisting of the twelve clubs at the meeting, with power to add to that number. Despite bitter protests from the smaller clubs who feared for their very existence if excluded from the proposed super-league, the big twelve forced through their resolution at an acrimonious management committee meeting held on June 4th, 1901. In fact, the first Northern Rugby League competition was played over the 1901/2 season Runaway first Champions were Broughton Rangers whose form was so outstanding that as early as February they could not be over-taken at the head of the league table. The 1902/3 season saw a further development in league football with the introduction of a two divisional system, eighteen teams in each division with promotion and relegation on a two-up and two-down basis at the end of each league season. This early venture had such a catastrophic effect on the gates of unsuccessful Second Division clubs that it was abandoned after only three seasons to be replaced by one division of 31 clubs with each club compiling its own fixture list. Though Leigh were declared champions as a result of topping the large shapeless league, many clubs complained that Leigh had provided themselves with an "easy" fixture list, ducking the challenge of the stronger clubs. Consequently a play-off formula was agreed for the following season (1906/7) according to which the top four clubs would be paired in semi-finals with the winners meeting on a neutral ground to decide the Championship.

It was also in the close season of 1906 that the Northern clubs took a decision establishing a fundamental and enduring difference between their game and traditional Rugby Union. For some years there had been an increasingly strong body of opinion which held that only a reduction in the number of players on the field would bring about the flowing, open play spectators thirsted after. It was generally agreed that the reduction should take place amongst the forwards though opinion was divided about how many forwards should disappear. Eventually a proposal by Warrington, seconded by Leigh, won the day, two forwards were dropped and teams reduced to 13 in number.

Thus in little more than a decade of astounding energy and unshakeable faith in their enterprise, the founding fathers of the Northern Union had developed a new game and established the structure of its competitions. The Northern League, the Championship Play-Off, and the Challenge Cup were contested before large crowds by teams playing 13-a-side Rugby and placing great emphasis on the basics of running, passing, and tacking.

Progressive and vigorous as they were, however, even those indefatigable gentlemen could not have anticipated the momentous developments about to take place.

A party of New Zealand businessmen following the famous 1905/6 All Blacks Rugby Union tour of Britain had taken the opportunity of watching some matches played in the rival code. They were much impressed with what they saw and decided to sponsor a New Zealand team on a tour of England, playing under Northern Union rules. The prime movers behind this bold and controversial enterprise were a Wellington business man, A. H. Baskerville, and George Smith, a top class New Zealand wing who had toured with the 1905 All Blacks. With their now customary zeal, the Northern Union administrators speedily concluded negotiations and in June 1907 they announced that a New Zealand team would visit Britain during the 1907/8 season. The tourists would receive 70% of gate receipts with minimum guarantees of £50 for mid-week matches and £100 for Saturday games. Smith was joined by fellow All-Blacks, Johnson, Mackrell, and McGregor. Also in the party were two youngsters destined to become legendary Rugby League figures – the Australian H. H. "Dally" Messenger, and the great Lance Todd. The "new-comers' performed very creditably, winning 19 out of 35 matches played, including two of the three Test Matches, and breaking even financially.

Meanwhile a break reminiscent of 1895 was about to take place in New Zealand's neighbour Australia. The New South Wales Rugby Union had grown militantly dissatisfied with rulings on broken time and compensation payments. At their invitation Baskerville's men had played three games in Sydney, attracting widespread interest. A momentous meeting followed at which the New South Wales President Mr. Harry Hoyle gave his casting vote in favour of a proposal to break away from the Rugby Union and form a league based on Northern Union rules. Exactly a year after the New Zealand pioneers set sail for Britain the first Australian Northern Union tourists left Sydney in August 1908. In Britain they played an astounding total of 46 games winning 19 and drawing 6. Their play was less spectacular than Baskerville's New Zealanders and crowds were moderate. However the Northern Union had guaranteed the tour against financial loss and far from being discouraged the Australians immediately invited the British to tour in 1910. The first tour by Great Britain "Down Under" encompassing fourteen matches in Australia and four in New Zealand was a huge success both in playing and financial terms. In little more than three years of unparalleled activity the Northern Union game had been rooted in both Australia and New Zealand and the pattern of reciprocal visits between Britain and the antipodes firmly established. The Australians returned to Britain in 1911, winning two and drawing one of the three Tests, and Great Britain toured Australia and New

Zealand again in 1914, returning only weeks before the outbreak of the Great War.

The amazing success of the game in the southern hemisphere was not matched by further expansion at home. Vigorous efforts had been made to establish the Northern Union game in Wales. In 1907 Merthyr Tydfil and Ebbw Vale joined the Northern Union, followed a year later by Aberdare, Barry, Mid Rhondda and Treherbert. Then, as now, however, the traditional Rugby Union game was deeply rooted in the hearts of the Welsh Nation "almost a religion" as they say – and resistance to the new game was fanatical. By 1914 there existed no team playing Northern Union rules in Wales.

Nevertheless many fine Welsh players "went north" capitalising on their playing skills, to join the wealth of home grown northern talent and stars such as Todd, Devereux, Francis, Gilbert and Rosenfeld, signed from the Australian and New Zealand touring teams. Many people view the years immediately prior to World War One as the first golden era of the Rugby League game. Attendances were excellent, the play thrilling and spectacular, finding its perfect expression in Huddersfield's all-conquering side immortalised as "the team of all the talents" which in the 1914 to 1915 season won all four major competitions open to it – the Yorkshire League, the Yorkshire Cup, the League Championship and the Challenge Cup. Harold Wagstaffe skippered a side which had no weakness and possessed in flying Australian winger Albert Rosenfeld, a scoring machine par excellence. His eighty tries in the 1913 to 1914 season remains an all time record unlikely to be eclipsed.

Along with most other sporting bodies the Northern Union shared the common experience of extreme hardship and virtual cessation during the 1914–18 war and after the Armistice a great resurgence of popularity with a public which had been starved of entertainment during the dark war years. With characteristic enterprise the Northern Union men were on their way Down Under as early as April 1920 for a tour specifically designed to revive the game at international level. In this respect the trip was an outstanding success with a world record attendance of 67,859 watching Sydney take on the tourists at Sydney Cricket Ground in the opening match of the tour. Unlike the first decade of the century, however, the 1920's and 1930's were in the main a period of consolidation rather than expansion for the Rugby League game. Nevertheless there occurred three very important events which were to leave their permanent mark on the sport.

First at the AGM of 1922 the Northern Union changed its name to the Rugby Football League thus severing the last vestige of connection with the parent game.

Then, in 1928, the Rugby League Council made the bold but controversial decision to stage the game's showpiece, the Challenge Cup Final, at a venue outside the North, its traditional home. The Final was now attracting huge attendances each year and existing grounds were proving inadequate to accommodate the crowds. The search was narrowed to two prospective London venus, the Crystal Palace and the fine new Wembley Stadium, opened just four years earlier. The Chairman and Secretary were despatched to inspect both venues and their recommendation that Wembley should be hired was accepted by the Council. The intention was to make the Final an annual event in the national sporting calendar, to create a desire in as many people as possible to attend the match and, "to make it easy in a financial sense and convenient from a travelling point of view to get there". The first Wembley Final was played on May 4th, 1929, when 41,500 people paid £5,614 to see mighty Wigan beat home-spun Dewsbury by thirteen points to two. Apart from 1932, when the stadium was unavailable, and the years of the Second World War, Wembley had housed each subsequent Challenge Cup Final and witnessed many moments of unforgettable drama. As the progressive minds of 1928–29 had predicted the day has become a family festival with tens of thousands of Northern folk joining Rugby League.

In the early 1930s the French Rugby Union was embroiled in a domestic dispute which was to result in the development of Rugby League across the channel. Allegations of professionalism and transfer fees prompted the four Home Countries to sever relations with the French until the latter had solved their problems to the satisfaction of the Home Unions. Effectively banned from International competition, some French officials began to negotiate with the Council of the Rugby Football League as a result of which Great Britain played an exhibition match against the 1933 Australian Tourists in Paris on Sunday, December 31st, 1933. In the large and appreciative crowd was French Rugby Union Star Jean Galia. Within three months Galia assembled a team of eighteen French players who toured England playing matches at Leeds, Hull, Salford, Wigan and White City, London. On April 15th 1934 France played Great Britain in an "International Match" at the Buffalo Velodrone in Paris and that August at a historic meeting in Tolouse the "Ligue Française de Rugby à Treize" was formed with twelve founder member clubs drawn largely from the traditional Rugby Country of the South and South West. The game in France developed rapidly and received a great boost in 1937 with its admission to the Federation National Des Sports, giving Rugby League equality of status with other French sports after only three years in being.

It took the Second World War and a Nazi puppet Government to halt, temporarily, the progress of Rugby League in France. On December 29th, 1941, the Vichy Government under Marshall Pétain dissolved the French Rugby League and confiscated both its property and its funds. In Britain, however, the real war brought a truce to the cold war which had existed between the two codes of Rugby since 1895, when the Rugby Football Union granted permission for servicemen who had played Rugby League in civilian life, to play Rugby Union in the Forces. This "privilege" was extended to National Servicemen during the post-war years. Indeed, during the war, charity matches were actually played under Rugby Union rules between teams representing Rugby Football Union and the Rugby League, both, incidentally, resulting in narrow victories for the Rugby League sides.

The years following World War II were undoubtedly a

golden age for the game. Enthusiasm was sky high, and there was an abundance of players of surpassing class to thrill the enormous crowds. As enterprising as ever, and despite the immense difficulties in finding transport, the Rugby Football League immediately answered the call of Australia and New Zealand to mount a tour in the summer of 1946. The party travelled on the aircraft carrier, "Indomitable" and enjoyed a highly successful trip in every respect. Capacity attendances were achieved at three successive Wembley Finals (1949, 50 and 51) and French initiative saw the establishment of a World Cup Competition in 1954, a depleted Great Britain side being the improbable winners of the inaugural tournament.

Inevitably the boom years reached their end and in the late 1950s and throughout the 1960s Rugby League experienced, along with other major spectator sports, a steady but apparently inexorable decline in attendances, as social habits changed and the competition for people's time and money became hotter.

Rugby League sought answers in a number of ways. Radical rule changes were introduced to make the game more open and spectacular. Sunday games were first sanctioned in December 1967, and largely to avoid competing with local soccer teams, by the early 1970s, most Rugby League Clubs had elected to play their matches on Sundays as a matter of course. Enterprising clubs such as Salford and Warrington established lavish social facilities, restaurants, and bars, setting examples which many other clubs were to follow in providing much needed income seven days a week, not merely on a Saturday or Sunday afternoon. The competitive "bite" which Rugby League fans demand was assured when a two-division system was finally firmly established at the beginning of the 1973/74 season after it had been tried unsuccessfully in the seasons 1962/3 and 1963/4. However, without doubt the most important single factor in Rugby League's fight for survival was the advent of its T.V. Age. Today this fact is generally accepted, but it was hotly contested for many years after the Rugby League Council had taken the decision to allow the B.B.C. to transmit, live, 13 League matches during the 1958/59 season. prior to this, both B.B.C. and I.T.V. had televised occasional matches, the first Nationwide broadcast being the Great Britain v New Zealand Second Test at Swinton on November 10th, 1951, screened by the B.B.C. What is certain is that television has succeeded where all the valiant efforts since 1895 had sadly failed. It has made Rugby League a truly national game, with millions of viewers enjoying up to 25 matches each season on B.B.C's Saturday "Grandstand" programme, as well as the 12 matches screened on Tuesday nights in the B.B.C 2 Floodlit Trophy Competition, first played in 1965.

This very popular Competition was abandoned in 1979 after a magnificent Final in which Hull beat their Humberside rivals, Hull K.R., 13–3 before a competition record crowd of over 18,000 people. However, the second half of the 1980/81 season saw the return of Rugby League football to the screens of Independent Television, when eight League matches were very successfully covered by both York-shire and Granada TV.

In addition to producing substantial fees for Rugby League's member clubs, it is certain that the influence of television has had much to do with the advent of the three new professional clubs at Fulham, Cardiff, and Carlisle. Television has also produced other important benefits to the clubs in the forms of ground advertising, free kit, and, most vital of all, lucrative sponsored competitions.

The first of these, when sponsorship was in its infancy, was the John Player Trophy, first contested in the 1971/ 72 season as a new knock-out competition involving all thirty professional clubs and two amateur teams. Today, all major Rugby League competitions are sponsored: The Challenge Cup by the House of Three Fives; The League Competition and the Premiership Play-off by Slalom Lager; The Lancashire Cup by Forshaws Brewery; and the Yorkshire Cup by Websters Brewery. In all, these sponsored events currently offer over £250,000 each sea-son in prize money alone, impressive figures indeed for a game so often clothed in the past with a Cinderella image.

# 2
# AMATEUR RUGBY LEAGUE

Although it is true to say that public attention is inevitably centred on the exploits of the stars playing Rugby League at its highest level, the sport could not prosper without a healthy and dedicated amateur organisation, playing and serving simply from a deep love of the game. In this respect, the formation of the British Amateur Rugby League Association in Huddersfield in March 4th, 1973, was the most significant event in the history of Rugby League. In former years, Amateur Rugby League had been administered from the headquarters of the professional game in Leeds, and for many years it had been possible for the administrators at Chapeltown Road successfully to dispense this dual responsibility. After the Second World War, however, the increasing necessity to run the professional game on strict business lines made it extremely difficult to give the amateur sport the progressive and committed leadership it so badly needed. Not unreasonably, there was a powerful feeling within the amateur ranks that their affairs should be placed in the hands of those who thoroughly understood, and were totally involved in, the amateur game.

Initially, B.A.R.L.A. was branded a rebel organisation, likely to produce a split in Rugby League ranks as dangerous and as far reaching as the "great divide" of 1895. However, a change of administration at Rugby League headquarters brought a change of attitude. Within twelve months the Rugby League's almost total opposition had changed to one of unanimous support for the new autonomous amateur association and good relations were restored. Shortly after, B.A.R.L.A. was officially recognised as the National Governing Body for Amateur Rugby League Football in Great Britain by the Government, the Sports Council and the C.C.P.R., and the way was then clear for further acceleration of their progress.

B.A.R.L.A., with its unimpeachable amateur status, meant that it was now possible for the sport to qualify for grant aid from the Sports Council for the future development of the game.

Realising that the life blood of any sport flows from the youngsters, B.A.R.L.A. immediately set about implementing a highly successful youth policy with the result that youth rugby has increased ten-fold during the last four years. Rugby at the youth level was given a terrific boost when the Great Britain 'Under 18' youth team made a pioneering tour to Australia and New Zealand in the Summer of 1977. A year later it was the seniors' turn when a history-making tour to Papua New Guinea, Australia and New Zealand was mounted. Nine tough games were played on a tour lasting 38 days and covering over 30,000 miles. The visit to Papua New Guinea was the first tour undertaken by any sports governing body in the world – a truly memorable piece of Rugby League history. The tourists proved to be great ambassadors and crowd pleasers, attracting capacity attendances wherever they played.

For the Test Match at Port Moresby, there was a crowd of 15,000 the gates being closed two hours before kick-off. The tourists rose to the occasion magnificently winning the Test convincingly, 28–7.

Though it has never lacked dedicated workers at the grass roots level, unlike Rugby Union and Cricket for example, Rugby League has rarely numbered amongst its adherents, people in the professions and armed forces who could generate enthusiasm of the game in the four corners of the earth. This is why the development of the game in the universities is seen to be of paramount importance by the progressive B.A.R.L.A. officials.

The University and Colleges Rugby League was formed ten years ago by a group of enthusiasts at Leeds University. Today the game is played in some 30 universities and colleges, the latest recruits being Oxford

The "Highlanders" welcome the British Amateur Rugby League team to Mount Hagen, Papua New Guinea

University who took the Southern Amateur Rugby League title in only their second year of existence, and their arch rivals Cambridge University. The first ever Oxford v. Cambridge Rugby League game took place at Craven Cottage, Fulham on Sunday, April 26th, Oxford just running out winners in a splendid match by 16–9. The Universities & Colleges Rugby League is now officially recognised and supported by the Universities Athletic Union. Apart from extremely well organised League and knock-out Cup Competitions, an annual Inter-County match is played and the highlight of the season is the International against the French Universities representative side played alternately at venues in France and Great Britain.

Rugby League in the schools suffered grievously when

Secondary Education was re-organised on comprehensive lines during the 1960s. Small schools, famous for many years for their prowess at the game, disappeared virtually over-night to be replaced, in many cases, by a single institution whose senior staff had little time for, or knowledge of, the game. However, thanks to a reorganised and progressive National Coaching Scheme and the unabated enthusiasm of schoolmasters comprising the English Schools Rugby League, an autonomous body largely financed by the Rugby League, the game in the schools has made a vital resurgence. The highlight of the Schools calendar is undoubtedly the "Under 11" intertown match played at Wembley Stadium each year as a curtain raiser to the Challenge Cup Final. The presentation and the quality of play exhibited at this final event are of the very highest standard. The game is justly proud of its ability to offer an eleven year old schoolboy the opportunity of a Wembley appearance or an 18 year old youth player the prospect of an Australasian tour with B.A.R.L.A.

The aim of B.A.R.L.A. is simply to spread amateur Rugby League throughout the British Isles. They believe that the game should be a part and creator of community spirit, and they have set a date for the completion of the task – 1995, exactly 100 years after the birth of Rugby League, following the 'split' with Rugby Union. The missionary zeal with which everyone connected with the amateur game is pursuing this vision makes the objective a very realistic probability.

Indeed the future of Rugby League, at all its levels, has never appeared brighter or more secure. A vigorous multi-million pound business at the professional level, a healthy, skilful and rapidly expanding sport enjoyed by tens of thousands of amateurs and schoolboys, the game for which many forecast but a few months of flickering life in 1895, faces the 1980s with the utmost confidence in the certainty of its continued existence and growth.

# 3
# THE ORGANISATION AND THE REFEREES

Professional Rugby League is now a multi-million pound business and requires a Headquarters staff commensurate with such responsibilities. Since 1934, the game's Headquarters has been housed in an imposing building at 180, Chapeltown Road on the outskirts of Leeds. For many years immediately prior to the move the game was run from the home in nearby Grange Avenue of the then Secretary, the delightful Mr. John Wilson, whose daughter acted as his Personal Secretary. Though there have been notions from time to time of selling up the property at Chapeltown Road and moving further away from the bustling city of Leeds, for a game like Rugby League it is essential that the Headquarters staff in no way become remote from the people they serve. The function of the Administration is to serve the game of Rugby League football: the game is not run for the benefit of the Administration.

The present Administration consists of Mr D. S. Oxley (Secretary-General); Mr D. J. Howes (Public Relations Officer); Mr R. S. Davis (Finance Officer); Mr G. A. Keith (Administration Officer); with the necessary and appropriate Secretarial and Clerical back-up.

The governing body of the game of Rugby League is the Council to which each member club has the right to elect one representative. It is important to understand that the club representatives on the Council collectively form the game's government; they do not meet as delegates of their representative clubs. However, it is right, proper, and prudent that on matters of great importance to the clubs the Council, as governing body of the game,

Rugby League Secretary,
David Oxley

will always seek the views of the member clubs. It is
also right and proper that only the clubs voting through
their delegates at the Annual General Meeting held late
in June can alter or amend the Bye-laws through which
the game is governed. Council meetings are always
chaired by the current Chairman of the Council. The
present incumbent is Mr Bill Oxley, a former professional player from Barrow. The Chairman is elected to
serve for one year at the Annual General Meeting.

Inevitably, the game's wide-ranging business is undertaken by the various specialised Committees which have
responsibility for Finance; International affairs; Cup
Competitions; Rules Revision; League Competitions; Dis-
ciplinary matters; International Selection; Marketing;

Rugby League President,
Lord Derby

Coaching; and the Under-19 (Colts) and Under-17 (Youth League) Competitions. When urgent business arises for which it would be impossible to assemble the whole Council, the Consultative Committee, consisting of the current Chairman, the Chairman elect, and the immediate past Chairman, is empowered to act on behalf of the Council.

The Cumbria, Lancashire, and Yorkshire County Rugby Leagues are autonomous bodies having their own Committees, Presidents, and Secretaries. Their function is to organise the County Cup Competitions and the annual County Championship matches. The Lancashire Combination and the Yorkshire Senior Competition are run by the relevant Committees and involve the reserve teams of the senior professional clubs.

All the Committees throughout the Rugby League are unpaid and few members even bother to claim expenses. The money to run the central administration at Chapeltown Road comes almost entirely from the proceeds of the Wembley Challenge Cup Final. This season's Final will gross some £700,000 if all tickets are sold. Of this vast sum, 30% goes to the Wembley Stadium Company as hire fee; 15% V.A.T.; 10% into the Cup Pool; and 10% to each of the Finalists. Substantial Grants are made to the Schools and Universities from the residue, so it can be seen that the Secretary-General must run a "tight ship" at Rugby League Headquarters.

The amateur game has its own full-time central staff under National Administrator, Maurice Oldroyd, with offices at Huddersfield, appropriately enough the cradle of the game.

At most of the professional clubs the vital need has been recognised of employing first rate full-time administrators and people specialising in the commercial developments which are such a vital component of each club's life-blood. Club Directors cannot be paid and, indeed, often have to dig deep into their own pockets to maintain solvency at their clubs.

While it has always been a sensible axiom of Rugby League government that the job should be done with the minimum possible staff necessary to ensure maximum efficiency, so rapidly is the game advancing that increases in the Central Administration are inevitable. A full-time Coaching Organiser is badly needed and the right man is sought to take charge of the vital area of recruiting, developing, training, and assessing the game's Referees.

As is the case with all "men in the middle", Rugby League Referees have to be enthusiasts with a deep love of the game. The rewards, at least in kind, are modest enough compared with the dedication and responsibility the job demands and the controversy it inevitably from time to time arouses.

A young man wishing to become a Rugby League Referee would normally apply to join his local District Society. There he will receive tuition in the basic skills of refereeing under the tutelage of more senior and experienced Referees. Eventually, after he has gained experience in the middle, his District Society may recommend him to take Rugby League's Referees' Examination which is held each Summer. Only 1 in 3 of all candidates are successful in achieving the required pass mark, in the region of 85%. Successful candidates become graded Referees joining the "ladder" on its lowest rung, Grade V. This means a Referee may officiate in the middle at reserve team games and in the Colts and Youth Leagues, and also run the line in First Team matches. Promising material amongst Grade V Referees may eventually be recommended by their County Society or by Rugby League's two Referees' Assessors, Messrs. Sam Shepherd and Joe Manley, who were, themselves, Senior Referees of great renown, to join the small band of Probationary Referees, whose performance will be closely monitored by the two Assessors with a view to their joining the Senior List of Referees at Grade II level. The best Grade II men are eventually promoted to Grade I status. At present there are 15 Grade I Referees and 8 having Grade II status. These Senior Referees officiate at First Team level and the International Panel is drawn from those having Grade I status. The Senior Referees have their own Association and meet regularly to seek ways of improving their performance and professional standing. In addition to refereeing First Team matches, however, many Senior Referees take charge of amateur and schoolboy matches, involving themselves in the Coaching Scheme and regularly attending the meetings of both their District and County Societies where their wealth of experience is, of course, invaluable.

The current remuneration for a Senior Referee in charge of a First Team game is £24 match fee, plus allowances for travelling and subsistence. At International level, the match fee is £50. A regular Referee Exchange system is operated in conjunction with the French League and the very best British Referees travel to Australia and New Zealand to take charge of matches Down Under.

In order to maintain the high standard of fitness required to take charge of today's top matches, all Senior Referees have to undergo demanding physical fitness tests conducted by the Human Performance Laboratory at Salford University three times each season. If any Senior Referee does not pass at any one time then he is not offered appointments until he has achieved the required fitness standard.

Like all sports these days, Rugby League finds it difficult to attract young people to take up the demanding job in the middle. To this end two famous former Senior Referees, Eric Clay and Mick Naughton, have recently been appointed Recruitment & Development Officers. The calibre of the men looked for must be of the highest, for many Senior Referees with long experience in the game tell me the job has never been harder. The six-tackle game makes very heavy demands on the Referee's fitness as the ball is swept from end to end of the field; these days every professional Rugby League game is a battle in the promotion or relegation stakes or a Cup tie involving a great deal of prize money; and in Rugby League, as in the wider world outside, there are signs of an erosion of the old fashioned respect for authority though, in general, the game can still be very proud of the discipline and self-control displayed by its players.

Within 14 days of each game the two clubs concerned

Oldham referee Sam Shepherd, now one of Rugby League's referee assessors, watches as Salford's Jackie Brennan sets himself to tackle a Dewsbury forward at Crown Flatt, Dewsbury. Alan McInnes (right) was a Salford capture from Sale Rugby Union club.

must forward to Rugby League Headquarters a comprehensive report on the Referee's performance, awarding him marks on the various sections which go to make up the skills required by a successful Referee: Application of Laws and Control (20); Positioning and Fitness (10); Stoppages and Signals (10); and General Performance (10). This, at first sight, might seem to be a very unsatisfactory system with vested interest playing far too big part. However, the actual marking is amazingly honest and it is by no means unusual for a club that has lost a game to give a Referee a glowing report or one that has won to show extreme dissatisfaction with the performance of the man in the middle!

## Rugby League Referees

Referees, like players, come in all shapes and sizes but they have in common a thick skin and a strong personality. Indeed, many of the game's outstanding characters have been found in the ranks of its Referees.

The first referee to take charge of a Challenge Cup final was J. H. Smith from Widnes. In 1900 a referee called Frank Renton came on to the scene and made his presence felt. He wore knickerbockers and stood out as a personality. He took charge of the 1900 Challenge Cup final when Swinton beat Salford. He continued to be a top referee and had many honours including Challenge Cup finals in 1907 and 1921. Frank Renton was from Hunslet which did not produce many top referees. Mr J. F. May (St Helens), Mr J. Bruckshaw (Stockport), Mr J. Kidd (Millom), Mr W. McCutchton (Oldham), Mr Marshall and Mr Robinson from Bradford were referees in the early days who officiated at Challenge Cup finals. Only the older followers of Rugby League will remember these names but they helped to make history.

A Methodist minister, the Reverend Frank Chambers arrived on the scene as a referee after playing with Huddersfield. He was in charge of the 1924 Challenge Cup final between Wigan and Oldham.

The Reverend Frank was a remarkable character both as a referee and a united Methodist minister. He was a forward of considerable strength and skill, I am told. I remember being taken to a Salem Chapel to hear the Reverend Frank leading a sportsman's service. When he left Huddersfield and retired down south I remember meeting him in Plymouth when I was with the 'Great Britain' Rugby League party sailing on the aircraft carrier the 'Indomitable' on the first post-war tour to Australia and New Zealand.

In the thirties quite a number of referees came into prominence. Frank Peel, father and son, were top whistlers, so was Frank Fairhurst (Wigan), and Albert Dobson, the smallest referee, yet very efficient who had two 'Wembley', finals, 1936 and 1946.

Warrington never really forgave 'Dobby' for the early try in 1936 by Isaacs, the Leeds loose forward, who they claimed was off side from an Eric Harris cross kick. In the forties George Phillips became one of the top 'Whistlers' and he had charge of a number of Cup finals and top matches. He was from Widnes and the 'Chemics' have provided quite a large number of good referees. One of the present top three referees is Mick Naughton from Widnes.

Jack Eddon, later to become a Swinton Club official was in the top bracket as a referee. Paul Cowell from Warrington near to Widnes had a lot of big matches in the middle. So did Alf Hill and Matt Coates from Dewsbury.

Charlie Appleton from Warrington – how often this area of West Lancashire comes into view – had a long run of big matches.

'Sergeant Major' Eric Clay came onto the scene in the sixties and seventies. I christened Eric 'Sergeant Major' for he had been in the services. He refereed a lot of top class matches including a stormy wild match against the Australians, at Headingley. He is still a strong supporter of Rugby League.

Other referees who hit the headlines with a Wembley appearance include Ron Gelder, who was the man in the middle for the Halifax-Warrington final first at Wembley and then at Odsal when the four-all draw took a reply to Odsal Stadium with the 104,000 gate.

Stan Adams, a schoolmaster in Hull who produced many good schoolboy footballers, had a cup final. So did E. Lawrenson and Sam Shepherd (now a referee assessor).

Obviously an appearance at Wembley as a referee or touch judge is the highlight of a career. There have been many good referees who for varying reasons have not officiated at Wembley. George Wilson, Dewsbury for instance did not have a Wembley but was in charge of that wonderful match at Odsal Stadium when St Helens beat Hunslet by 44 pts to 22 pts and that included the famous Tom Vollenhoven try for St. Helens. Norman Railton and Joe Manley had championship match appearances, so did Dewsbury cum Blackpool referee, D. S. Brown, along with Harry Hunt, Matt Coates and others.

Being a Rugby League referee is a labour of love but the successful 'middle men' are always keen to help the newcomers as they start on grade five looking longingly at grade one and the twin spires of Wembley.

One thing I cannot recall is a top player becoming a top referee. Possibly they know the problems of the job!

## Personal Profile of a Top Referee – By himself

### William Henry (Billy) Thompson

Billy Thompson, a 45-year-old engineer with a Huddersfield-based tractor manufacturer, is a world leader in his own right. For most of the 1970s and initial period of 1980 he was rightly labelled as the world's best referee by the British authorities. This was based, soundly in my opinion, on his handling of all his matches and the fact that the Australians did not mind him taking the world championship final between them and the British in 1977.

Married with three daughters Billy could have been lost to professional soccer but for a lucky break. Actually the break was rather painful for Billy but Rugby League certainly benefited. He was about to sign professional terms with Third Division South Soccer club Gillingham, but after breaking a scaphoid bone in his hand he returned home to Huddersfield before he could sign. He had his arm in plaster for a year.

His return to Yorkshire saw him switch to Rugby League refering and by 1962 he passed the local referees' exam. Four years later he was promoted to grade two and twelve months after that he arrived at the top, grade one.

Straight-talking Billy is honest as the day is long. He readily admits that his worst ever display was in the 1969 championship final, Leeds v Castleford at Odsal, and says modestly: "The game may have come a little too early in my career.

"It was just one big fight and I must take some of the blame for allowing it to happen. Still some good did come out of that disaster. It taught me a great deal. I became a harder man and a much better referee."

Equally Thompson remembers what he considers to be the best game he ever controlled – the 1978 Challenge Cup final at Wembley between Leeds and St Helens. He recalled: "For 80 minutes both teams just threw the ball about in a bewildering fashion and it was an epic game."

Thompson's dry, laconic humour is known throughout the British professional game and a sparkle came to his eye when he brought to mind one particularly humourous moment from the thick of a battle.

"I was controlling a game between Rochdale Hornets and Halifax. After a tackle I retreated the necessary five yards and was lost for words when Rochdale hooker Kevin Ashcroft, who is now coach in Salford, said: 'If that's five yards Billy I wouldn't want you to fit a carpet for me!' "

Billy added: "I still smile to myself when I think of that moment. That, to me, illustrates why Rugby League is such a great game and shows perfectly the respect between our players and referees."

No referee in Rugby League progresses very far without having to send a player off the field. In a physical game like Rugby League tempers often boil over and referees are left with no other option but to send the offenders for the famous early bath.

Thompson admits to having issued the marching orders several times but the most famous dismissal of all must be when he gave Leeds centre Syd Hynes marching orders during the 1971 Wembly final against Leigh.

Test star Syd was involved in an off-the-ball incident with Leigh player-coach Alex Murphy and a touch judge intervened. Thompson said: "Nobody wants incidents like that to happen at Wembley, but I believe my decision was justified."

But nobody will ever convince Leeds fans that Murphy helped the situation along and that Hynes should not have been sent for that long walk to the dressing rooms. Thompson, meanwhile, added: "Although I've sent quite a few players off in my career it's not as many as people believe."

One method that Thompson uses to take the heat out of controversial incidents is to talk to players as the game progresses. He explained: "I believe this assists the continuity of the game and helps stop you blowing the whistle too often. And there are quite a number of times when it pays you to listen to certain players – and sometimes you don't have much option but to listen."

Retiring age for Rugby League referees is 50. Thompson is now 47 so he still has three good years left as a top referee.

Since Thompson made it to the top of the refereeing tree there have been many changes in the game of Rugby League. He has seen the introduction of the six tackle limitation, differential penalties, various scrummage changes and a whole host of other technical changes involving the reduction of drop goals from two points to one. But his affection for the game he found after finishing with soccer still remains and he said: "To me, it is still the finest and hardest ball game in the world."

And his affection for the sport has been returned with an honour strewn career that has seen him control Lancashire Cup finals, BBC-2 Floodlit Cup finals, World Cup games, Championship finals, Wembley Cup finals, Premiership finals, John Player Cup finals, numerous internationals and be named as the Trumann's Steel Referee of the Year on several occasions. Yes, Billy Thompson has made his mark on Rugby League.

# 4
# THE ENGLISH CLUBS

**Barrow Cumbria**
Name of ground. Craven St. Park. Colours. Royal Blue jersey with blue shorts. Former grounds. Cavendish Park and Little Park Roose. Record transfer fee £19,000 paid to Keith Jarrett, Newport Rugby Union and Welsh RU International 1969. Rugby League Challenge cup winners 1955. Runners up 1938 1951 and 1967. Club nickname 'Ship Builders'. Record attendance 21,651 in 1938 against Salford. A record of 50 tries was scored for the club by Jim Lewthwaite in 1956–1957. Willie Horne stand off half was one of the all time greats, with 298 points in season 51/52. Some names to remember:
Frank Castle winger, Bryn Knowlden centre, Phil Jackson, Dennis Goodwin, Reg Parker, Bill Burgess, father and son, Tom Brophy, Jack Grundy.

**Batley 'Gallant Youths'.**
Founder member R.L. Mount Pleasant. 'Gallant Youths'. Cerise and Fawn hooped jerseys and white shorts. First Challenge Cup winners in 1897, 1898 and 1901. The Mount Pleasant estate left to the town with conditions that no alcoholic liquor was to be served. For many years the cricket pavilion was used as dressing rooms for teams. The first cup winning team beating St Helens 8 to 3 was Garner, Wattie Davies, Dai Fitzgerald, Jim Goodall, I. Shaw, J. Oakland, H. Goodall, Mark Shackleton, Jim Gath, George Main, Bob Spurr, F. Fisher, C. Stabley, J. Littlewood and J. T. Numms. A dropped goal by Oakland counted 4 pts. Wilf Auty, later Mayor of Batley played in Batley's 1901 victory against Warrington. Some names to remember:

Harold Nujns, Mick Foley, Bill Hudson, C. Eaton, Eric Hesketh, George Davidges, Bryn Willians, Ike Fowler, Joe Robinson and Jack Perry. Ground capacity 20,000. Championship winners 1923/24.

### Blackpool Borough
Founded 1954. Borough Park, capacity 12,000. Tangerine jerseys with black and white band. Nickname 'Seasiders'. Biggest attendance 1957, 21,000 3rd RL Cup Blackpool v Leigh, played at Bloomfield Road ground,

### Bradford Northern
Has had a traumatic R.L. life. Playing at Park Avenue from 1895 to 1907, won the Challenge cup in 1906, then soccer took over. Moved to Birch Lane in 1908 and became known as 'T' Old Steam Pigs'. Had little success but made ambitious move to Odsal. Present champions of R.L. Under Harry Hornby and Dai Rees the club had its big success in the late forties and mid fifties. Welsh International Willie Davies from Swansea RU, teamed up with captain Ernest Ward, the best and perhaps smallest signing moneywise costing £150 from Dewsbury boys club. Frank Whitcombe and Trevor Foster good Welsh signings in the forwards. Played in three successive Wembly Finals 1947, 1948 and 1949 all captained by Ernest Ward. Disbanded in mid sixties but immediately reformed in 1964. Other good buys Joe Philips, McLean amongst half a dozen Kiwis signed. Have won the Rugby League Championship in successive seasons 1979-80, 1980-81 under dynamic coach Peter Fox.

### Bramley
Known as the 'Villagers'. Played at Barley Mow now known as McLaren Field. Greatest honour winning BBC floodlit competition at Widnes under daylight because of electricity power cuts in 1973. Loyal following in West Leeds. Ground record 1901 with 12,000. Ted Spillane of

New Zealand fame played scrum half and Bob Bartlett, Australia were star signings.

## Cardiff City

In May 1981 the Rugby League accepted an application for membership from Welsh soccer club Cardiff City. Clearly influenced by the success at Fulham and the decision of Carlisle to try and combine the two sports yet another attempt to establish the 13-a-side code in South Wales is in prospect.

Several previous South Wales based professional clubs were eventually forced to close because they lacked support from the Welsh public who were reluctant to shift their loyalty from their passion, Rugby Union.

While these words were being written famous Welsh Rugby names like Phil Bennett, Bobby Windsor, Graham Price and Paul Ringer from the Union world together with Jim Mills, Clive Griffiths and Brian Juliff from the League world were being strongly linked with the embryo Welsh Club. Much, however, will hang on whether David Watkins, the man given the task of selling League to the Welsh public, can succeed in his job as team supremo.

## Carlisle United

Inspired by the success of Fulham's combination of Football League soccer and Rugby League, Carlisle successfully applied for membership of the 13-a-side code before the end of the 1980–81 campaign. They will, however, not start operations until 1981–82.

Their search for Rugby success was based on very similar lines to Fulham with the appointment of a proven former Rugby League administrator, former Workington Town chairman George Graham, together with a player-coach Alan Agar, who joined them from Wakefield Trinity.

Agar's organisational ability has been proved on the field many times especially during his spells with Hull

Alex Murphy, rated by many to be the best RL player of all time. After playing career with St. Helens he moved to be player-coach of Leigh and then Warrington. Later he went as coach to Salford and then back to Leigh. Controversial man in every respect.

KR, when they won the Challenge Cup in 1980, and with Wakefield Trinity during their championship bid in 1980–81. His assistant is another popular Yorkshire-based player Mike Morgan, who captained Featherstone Rovers in 1980–81.

Carlisle's chances of League success must be viewed in relation to their geographical position. They are close to existing Rugby League territory in Cumbria and handily placed to recruit from Rugby Union in the South of Scotland. Big crowds, however, are not likely to be regular features unless they can produce a winning team straight away. The sparsely populated border country does not tolerate failure easily.

Syd Hynes, now coach of Leeds, launches another attack during his playing days at Headingley. Watching him is the then Castleford forward Ian Van Bellen.

### Castleford

Joined the league in 1926. Colours yellow jersey with black collar and cuffs with black shorts. First winner of BBC 2 floodlit competition 1966, 1967 and 1968. R.L. cup winners 1935, 1969 and 1970. Mainly home grown players including Alan Hardisty, Keith Hepworth, 'Bruss' Atkinson, Bernard Cunniffe, Jim Croston and Albert Lunn. Forwards, McManus, Smith, Taylor and Crossley. The club's first press box was the top deck of a tram. Bottom deck used as tea room. Club has now a VIP lounge. Ground at Wheldon Road and nickname 'Glassblowers'.

### Dewsbury

First team to qualify for the first Challenge Cup final at Wembley in 1929 v. Wigan who had drawn the semi-final game against St Helens. Lost the 1929 Final at Wembley but won the Challenge Cup in 1912 and 1943.

Welshman Dai Thomas holds try scoring record for the club with 40 tries. Colours red amber and black. Name of ground Crown Flatt, which has a slope to one corner known as 'Nine hole'. First famous player named with club was 'Dickie' Lockwood, others to follow Billy Rhodes, Joe Lyman, Cliff Smith, Jim Ledgard, Charlie Seeling, Frank Gallagher, Mick Stephenson sold for record £20,000 to Australian club Penrith.

### Doncaster

RLFC were founded in 1951 and first played at the local Greyhound Stadium. They borrowed some players from nearby Castleford, Hunslet and Leeds clubs and had a successful start. They moved to their own ground named Tattersfield after the chairman at that time. Bryn Goldswain had a successful period as coach after his playing career with Oldham. Mervyn Hicks was their costliest signing from Warrington. They have not won any honours as yet but recent signs have indicated they are capable of surprises. Colours white jerseys with blue and gold bands.

### Featherstone Rovers

With the lowest population of any League club Featherstone have produced many great footballers, with gates larger than the population of the town. They joined the league in 1921 and have won the Challenge Cup, the Yorkshire cup and runners-up in the League Championship. They have a small ground, Post Office Road, and very loyal followers. Appear to be able to find good scrum halves. Steve Nash, Britain scrum half now with Salford, is one of many finds from Featherstone. Others include Carl Dooler, Tommy Smales, Harold Moxon and Don Fox. Forwards are a natural product, like coal, with many fine forwards including Jimmie Thompson, Keith Bridges, Mal Dixon etc. Colours are blue and white hooped jerseys with navy blue shorts.

### Fulham

Fulham became members of the Rugby League in time for the start of the 1980–81 season. Their birth as partners with Third Division soccer at famous West London stadium Craven Cottage was the brain-child of their club chairman Mr Ernie Clay.

He wanted the Craven Cottage facilities to be utilised more and decided to run a Rugby League side in conjunction with soccer. Although Rugby League is played on an amateur basis in London, the professional game had never really caught on despite two experiments before the Second World War.

Mr Clay's belief in Rugby League appears to have paid off for they achieved promotion to the First Division at their first attempt and attracted impressive crowds to all their first season home games.

Much of the credit for that success, however, can also be placed at the feet of Rugby director Harold Genders, a former player who joined the Craven Cottage board from a similar position at Warrington. It was he who engineered the signing of player-coach Reg Bowden, an international class scrum half, from Widnes for £30,000, and together they have forged an impressive club side. Their test, however, will be to achieve similar good results against better quality First Division opposition in 1981–82. And that's not going to be easy.

### Halifax

R.L. cup winners 1903, 1904, 1931 and 1939. Won the first John Player trophy competition in 1972. The clubs last prewar Wembley success was in 1939 when they had a staggering success beating Salford by 20 pts to 3. Hubert Lockwood, later to become the Chairman of the

Rugby League, kicked four goals, with tries by Welshman Bevan New Zealander Smith and Treen and Todd.
Easy Wembley win against York in 3rd Wembley, winning by 22 pts to 8. Biggest attendance at any R.L. match
was when Halifax played Warrington in 1954 cup final
replay. 4–4 at Wembley replay at Odsal stadium before
a world record crowd of 104,000. Relegated at the end of
1980–81 after just one season in the First Division.
Ground, Thrum Hall, colours, blue and white hooped
jerseys with white shorts.

The late Dave Valentine.
Joined Huddersfield
from Hawick RU club in
Scotland. Led a team of
no-hopers to win first RL
World Cup in France in
1954.

## Huddersfield

With claret and gold jerseys they play at Fartown. Once
described as a team of all talents, although now they
have problems and are in the second division. It was in
Huddersfield that the breakaway from Rugby Union
came about.

With a mixture of Welshmen, Australians, New Zealanders and Yorkshiremen, Huddersfield were regularly
amongst the cup winners until a decade ago.

Harold Wagstaffe, regarded as the all time great,
joined Fartown as a boy of 16 years and became a folk
hero. With Australian Albert Rosenfeld on the wing, he
scored 80 tries in a season, a record which still stands.
Other Australians: Lionel Cooper, John Hunter, Ron
Bailey, Ernie Mills, Ray Markham and Welshmen:
Johnny Rogers and Ben Gronow plus Yorkshireman:
Mike Sullivan.

## Hull

Their ground is 'The Boulevard'. Only one Challenge
Cup final win in 1914. Since then they have had seven
appearances including two at Wembley without success.
Famous names led by Billie Batten included World War
One VC Jack Harrison who scored 52 tries in season
1914/15. Five championship wins. Coaches in fifties and
sixties by Roy Francis, who produced one of the best
packs of forwards, Scott, Harris, Drake (Jim), Sykes, and
Whiteley. Popular stand known as 'threepenny stand'.
Team known as 'Airlie Birds'. Cup finalists in 1980 when

Hull Kingston Rovers v. York. Harry Bath Rovers RU convert tries to stay in play against the weight of a York trio.

they were beaten by Hull KR, they are now a major power in the game with a team that includes many internationals. Colours, irregular black and white hooped jerseys.

## Hull Kingston Rovers

They have won all trophies including Challenge Cup 1979/80; they played at Wembley in 1964 captained by the late Harry Poole but lost to Widnes 13 points to 5 points. Graham Paul from Penzance christened the "Cornish Express" scored many spectacular tries. In the early years 'Tich' West scored a record 53 points against Cumberland club, Brookland Rovers. Known as the 'Robins' player coach Roger Milward has had great success and in 1977 Hull K R won the BBC trophy against St Helens in a brilliant match. This was the club's first trophy in 25 years. Amongst names to recall are Arthur Moore, "Scrubber" Dale, "Bunker" Carmichael, Jack Feetham, Ted Tatersfield, Laurie Osborne, Bielby and Boagey.

They were beaten 18-9 by Widnes in the 1980-81 final at Wembley. Ground, Craven Park, colours, white jerseys with red band.

Hull versus York, 1981.
Sammy Lloyd is tackled.

### Huyton

Huyton near Liverpool is an off shoot of clubs like Wigan Highfield, London Highfield, Liverpool Stanley and Liverpool City. The club has had a hard road to survive but has had some good coaches, Dave Cox, Coan Joe, and Jack Broome. When under the banner of Wigan Highfield they had reared many local players including Jack Maloney and Billy Belshaw and occasionally startled big brother from the other end of Wigan. Survival is the main aim for Huyton at this moment. Ground, Alt Park, colours, scarlet jerseys, sky blue shorts.

### Keighley

Overlooking Ilkley Moor, the ground has been described as the prettiest in the Rugby League. Keighley have never won the Challenge Cup or the Yorkshire county cup, yet have given a lot of support to the code. The ground, called Lawkholme Lane, has had 14,000 spectators at a cup tie. The nearest cup success came in 1937 when they met Widnes at Wembley. Keighley had a mixture of nationalities led by Welshman scrum half Dai Davies. Reg Lloyd was for many years the youngest player to appear at Wembley, in fact he might still have that honour. He scored Keighley's only try. Idris Towill and Gwyn Parker were the centres and a strong pack of different nationalities Traill, Halliday, Jones, Dixon, Talbot and Gill will be remembered. A colourful jersey with scarlet and emerald green V in white jersey. Brian Jefferson holds the club points record with 331 in season 1973/74.

### Leeds

Leeds won the R. L. Challenge Cup for the first time in 1910 and have at fairly regularly intervals repeated the success. It has a penchant for Welshmen and Australians with an occasional New Zealander player like Bert Cook. One of the best signing from Sydney was Arthur Clubes the big forward, who has stayed in England with Cook. "Dinny" Cambell was one of the early Australian signings and at regular intervals players from the antipodes

Opposite: Hull Kingston Rovers versus Hull in the 1980 final. Roger Millward with the cup.

Martin Ryan.
One of the all time great
full-backs.

came to Headingley as Vic Hey ("Chimy" Busch, Ted Verrenkamp, Jeff Moores became favourites). Welshmen were many and included the big point scorer Lewis Jones. Half back Oliver Morris was killed in the war and Dickie Williams who captained Great Britain in Australia were names still remembered and the deeds still recalled. There is also a strong local element of home produced players in the club's history: "Juicy" Adams, Syd Hynes, John Atkinson, Mick Shoebottom, John Holmes, Charlie Eaton. Colours are blue and gold.

**Leigh**
Leigh staggered the Rugby League world in 1961 when they signed Bev Risman son of the famous Gus for £6,500. Risman was a Union International who later moved to Leeds. For many years the club played at Mather Lane a ground I remember but they had had many grounds for Rugby before my time. They now play at Hilton Park named after a Leigh club chairman James Hilton who with my help produced a big sensation when Australian Trevor Allen, a Rugby Union centre, signed Macdonald Bailey, the sprint champion. The biggest local signing was Alex Murphy who led them to the first Wembley win against Leeds when Syd Hynes of Leeds was sent off. In Leigh's first Challenge Cup success when they beat Halifax 13 nil, they had Clarkson at full back with a small stocky scrum half called Walt Mooney and prominent forwards including J. Darwell and J. Cartwright.

**New Hunslet (now called just Hunslet)**
One of the most recent clubs to join the Rugby League is New Hunslet. After the Hunslet club who played at Parkside left the league a New Hunslet club was formed in 1973. They leased the Elland Road greyhound stadium and surprised a lot of cynics by not only surviving but creating a new following in a Leeds stadium opposite the Leeds United AFC ground. They made their presence felt very soon by putting up some unusual goal posts in

the shape of a letter Y. Eventually they were asked to conform to the normal rugby goal posts which they did but they had brought the club to the attention of the media. Chairman of the club, Ron Teeman and directors Gordon Murray and Jerry Mason, reckon that trophy success is not far away. Colours green and white. Promotion to Division One but after differences with the greyhound company they had to leave the stadium and are now looking for a site. At the moment they share Mount Pleasant with Batley.

### Oldham

Half way up the Pennines, Oldham have four covered stands at their Watersheddings ground. The club's nickname is 'Roughyeds', nothing to do with rough play. They have never played at Wembley in a cup final but have won the cup on three occasions. They played in four successive finals. In 1924 against Wigan they lost 21 pts to 4 pts. In 1925 beat Hull KR. 16–3. In 1926 they lost to Swinton 9 pts to 3 but levelled the score when a year later in 1927, they defeated Swinton 26 pts to 7. George Hesketh, the scrum half, played in all four finals, as did Bob Sloman and Sid Rix and Albert Brough. A winger of Italian extraction, Jack Corsi, one of a number of brothers, scored in two of the finals he played in. Although that flush of four successive Challenge Cup finals were the last Oldham played in, they had a lot of trophy success in the mid-fifties when Bernard Ganley, John Etty, Alan Davies and Ike Southward were prominent. Southward's transfer from Cumberland cost £10,000.

### Rochdale Hornets

Staged a most important match at their Athletic Grounds in 1930 when England won the Ashes with a try by Leeds winger Stan Smith and a score of 3 pts to nil. Harry Sunderland, the Australian manager, had asked for an extra match and he got it, but not the Ashes. Rochdale were one of the first to sign Rugby Union players from Fiji. In their one and only Challenge Cup

Welshman Alan Davies, centre star for Great Britain and championship winning Oldham team of the 1950s.

success against Hull in 1922 they had two Corsi brothers, one on the wing and the other in the forwards. Amongst the first Rochdale records were 109 goals in a season, kicked by Walt Gowers, father of Ken, who played for Swinton in the 1950s and 1960s. Both father and son toured Australia, father on the 1928 tour and Ken on the 1966 tour. In season 66/67 Graham Starkey scored nearly 250 points for Rochdale. Other Rochdale players who toured Australia include J. Robinson, W. Roman 1914, J. Bowers 1920, J. Bennett 1924, E. Cahill 1954. Their colours are red, white and blue.

### St Helens

A shock defeat at Wembley in 1930 by Widnes has been fully compensated by fine achievements in all competitions by the Saints, with wins at Wembley in 1956, 1961, 1966, 1972 and 1976. BBC 2 trophy winners in 1971 and 1975 and many successes in the Lancashire County cup and premiership in 1976. A galaxy of talents, both home grown like Alex Murphy and many others, coupled with some fruitful signings like Tom Van Vollenhoven, the greatest ever winger in the eyes of Saints fans, and Len Killeen. Under astute coaching first, with Jim Sullivan and later with Eric Ashton, many players have matured at Knowsley Road. The 1930 Cup final defeat had some consolation when the Saints beat Leeds in 1931 in the top four play-off and then Huddersfield 9 pts to 5 to take the Championship. New Zealand winger Roy Hardgrave was in the successful side, along with Tom Winnard, George Lewis, H. Frodsham, Jack Arkwright. Colours, white jerseys with red V.

### Salford

Named "Red Devils" by France. The ground is called "The Willows" Their colours are red jerseys and white shorts.

A record signing fee of £15,000 was paid to David Watkins when he signed professional from Newport and Wales Rugby Union. In the club's early days the most famous name was James Lomas. Lance Todd managed Salford for a period with many championship and country successes. Amongst many star signings were Alan Edwards, Sammy Miller, Tom Kenny, Keith Fielding, Barney Hudson, Emlyn Jenkins, Bert Day, Billie Williams, Tom Danby, George Curran, Cliff Evans, Chris Hesketh.

## Swinton

Known as the "Lions", the ground is in Station Road, Swinton, near Manchester. The ground capacity is 35,000. It has been used for many big matches including Test Matches against the Australians. The Kangaroos still talk about a disallowed try in a Test Match in 1929 when the match ended in a draw. In the replay England won by one try to nil, scored by Stanley Smith at Rochdale. Gate record 44,621 v Leigh (Lancashire cup final 1951). Amongst outstanding players were half backs Welshmen Billo Rees and Bryn Evans. Always a good pack outstanding in the thirties with players like Martin Hodgson, goal kicker Butters and Beswick. More modern

John Mantle of St. Helens, Wales and Great Britain makes a break during his early days at Knowlsey Road in a match against Barrow.

Alan Agar (r) joins Keith Rayne and Terry Day in defensive action for Wakefield Trinity against Halifax, 1981.

stars include Ken Gowers, full back, and forward Dave Robinson. Colours, blue jerseys with white V.

## Wakefield Trinity

Colours white, with red and blue hoops. The ground is called Belle Vue. Started its life via the Young Men's society connected with Holy Trinity Church. A long list of local players produced, including the famous Jonty Parkin, a scrum half who captained England successfully. After a long spell with Trinity he bought his own transfer for £100 and moved to Hull Kingston Rovers where he founded a successful fish business. H. Kershaw, T. Poynton, T. Newbould and Jonty Parkin played in the early tours in Australia, to be followed by the two Pollards, Charlie and Ernest, Bill Horton, Gilbert Robinson,

G. H. Exley, H. Murphy, D. Turner, Neil Fox, Harold Poyton, Gerry Round and Jack Wilkinson. Wakefield met Wigan in the first 1946 post-war cup final at Wembley, when Billy Stott kicked a dramatic goal near to time to win the cup. Beaten by Widnes in the 1979 Challenge Cup Final at Wembley.

Warrington defenders crash down St. Helens winger Frank Wilson Parry Gordon ducks a hand off to assist winger Brian Glover. St. Helens v Warrington 1969.

## Warrington

Founder member of the Rugby League, known as the 'Wires'. Colours are white jersey with primrose and blue band. Provided the game with one of the greatest wing threequarters when they signed Australian Brian Bevan after he had been turned down by Leeds. Bevan's record of around 800 tries is an all time try-scoring record. The name of their ground is 'Wilderspool', with covered stands on all four sides, and includes a restaurant from which the match can be seen. Their many signings include Harry Bath, an Australian, first signed by Barrow. The New Zealand stand off Ces Mountford had a successful time with Warrington. Other stars include Ally Naughton, John Bevan Welsh RU International, Bryn Knowlden, Gerry Helme, Jim Challinor (also with Barrow), Ray Price, Harold Palin, Bill Shankland, golfer too, Billie Dingsdale, and in the 1905 and 1907 cup final, Jack Fish.

### Whitehaven

Founded in 1948. Colours are chocolate, blue and gold hoops on white jersey. Recreation Ground. As yet have not won any trophies but came near to a Wembley appearance in 1957 when they held the mighty Leeds at Bradford in the Challenge Cup semi-final only to be thwarted with a long drop goal by Jeff Stevenson. One of the best ever full backs, Jim Brough, coached the club for a spell. Other coaches have been Eppy Gibson, Sol Roper and Ron Morgan. Most of its players come from the famous breeding grounds in the villages around Whitehaven, with Kells, the town on the hill-top, being one of the most prolific sources.

### Widnes

Founded in 1895. Colours black and white. Ground at Naughton Park. Known as the "Chemics", with a ground capacity 25,000 until recently. Mainly home produced. Their first success was dramatic when they beat St Helens, a team of many stars, at Wembley in 1930 by 10 pts to 3 pts. It was an all local Widnes team apart from G. van Rooyen, a South African. The seventies have provided Widnes with their most successful period and the club, whilst keeping their local products, have been willing to spend. Local born stars include Frank Myler, Nat Silcock, Jim Hoey, Harry Dawson, Ray Dutton, Vince Karalius, Reg Bowden.

Recent successful signings from Rugby Union include Mick Burke, who won the Lance Todd Trophy man of the match award in Widnes' 18-9 win over Hull KR at Wembley in 1981. He scored a try and kicked four goals.

Frank Myler of Widnes and St. Helens shows his style when playing for the Chemics (Widnes) in a match against Hull KR.

Widnes . . . Cup heroes of the 1970s. Team picture circa 1975.

Widnes versus
Warrington in the 1981
semi-final.

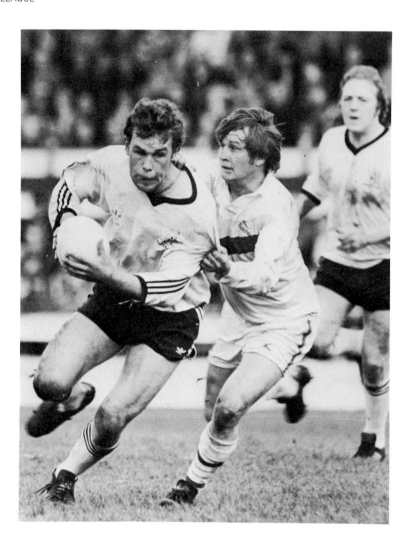

### Wigan

Founder member of the Rugby League. Known throughout the sporting world as one of the 'great' clubs. Many
honours in all competitions. The first Challenge cup success was in 1924 and the first championship success was
in 1909. The ground, Central Park, held 48,000 at a St
Helens league match in 1957. An enterprising club when
it comes to signing players in any part of the rugby
playing world. The immortal Jim Sullivan, who passed
away in 1978 and scored over 6000 points, heads a most

impressive list, which includes Charles Seeling, Ces Mountford, Brian Nordgren, E. Watkins, Welshmen galore amongst a galaxy of talent, Ted Ward, Danny Hurcombe, Billy Boston, John Ring, and home grown stars, Joe Egan, George Hesketh, Jack Cunliffe, Eric Ashton, Tom Bradshaw, Jack Hilton, Brian McTigue, David Bolton.

South Africa provided Van Rooyen and Van Heerdon. Wigan was relegated to the Second Division in 1979-80 but won promotion at the first attempt in 1980-81.

Widnes v Hull Kingston Rovers, 1981 Cup Final Les Gorley is stopped.

Eric Ashton one of the most stylish centres ever. Played for Wigan and Great Britain. Coaches Wigan, Leeds, St. Helens and Great Britain.

## Workington Town

Ground, Derwent Park, founded in 1944. Its great years were in the mid fifties when it won the Challenge Cup at Wembley in 1952. Runners up in 1955 and 1958. Winners of the championship 1950/51 and runners up 1957/8. Lancashire cup winners in 1977 and runners up in 1978. Nucleus of players recruited from the great amateur feeding ground in Cumbria. An enterprising club which brought Australian stars to the club including Rupert Mudge, Tony Paskins; local boys who made good in the big time included Eppy Gibson, Albert Pepperell, Billy Ivison, Ike Southward, Brian Edgar, Ces Thompson, and Andy Key and many others, not forgetting the guiding hand in the years of glory at Workington, the famous Gus Risman. Colours white jersey with blue band. The club was relegated to the Second Division in 1980-81.

## York

Ground, Wiggington Road. One of the prettiest grounds in the league. Capacity full stretch 20,000. Stands on both sides of the ground. Progressive club, who have never won the Challenge Cup, but were runners up in the Wembley final in 1931 against Halifax, when they had nine Welshmen playing in the team. Colours amber and black. Coaches at the club have included former internationals like Dai Prosser, Tommy Harris, Ernest Pollard, Laurie Gant. In the mid twenties they had a number of policeman playing with the team. Known as the Minster Men; winners Yorkshire Cup 1922, 1933 and 1936. They moved back into the First Division in style in 1980-81, being promoted as Second Division Champions.

Widnes v Hull Kingston Rovers, 1981 Cup Final Mick George scores Widnes's second try.

# 5
# THE WORLD CUP

In 1954, when the tour to Australia and New Zealand had just ended, many British players said no to the invitation to take a trip across the Channel to play against the best of Australia, New Zealand and France in the first World Cup series. The result was that the Kangaroos, having just beaten Great Britain in Test football in Sydney, were hot favourites.

Paris was the first World Cup match venue and New Zealand met France there on the last Saturday in October. By half-time France were in front by 12 points to 8. A big heavyweight forward, J. Delaye, had crashed his seventeen stone through the New Zealand defence for a vital try that enabled France to go to the dressing-room with the pleasant expectation that the next try would be the likely winner. And so it proved when Jo Crespo scored, putting France one up in the tournament.

Great Britain had a really mixed bag of players in their party, some with experience, some newcomers and some in doubtful condition. Dave Valentine, of Huddersfield and Hawick fame, was skipper and drilled his men on team spirit. Among other things he taught them to sing a Mctavish song of Scots lowland fighting!

The thirteen selected to do duty for Great Britain against Australia in Lyons were Jimmy Ledgard, David Rose, Phil Jackson, Mick Sullivan and Frank Kitchen; Gordon Brown and Gerry Helme; John Thorley, Sam Smith, Bob Coverdale, Basil Watts, Don Robinson and Dave Valentine.

Clive Churchill, whom I had seen carried shoulder-high from the Sydney cricket ground some years earlier,

Mick Sullivan immortal
Great Britain winger
with Huddersfield and
Wigan. Made comeback
to lead Dewsbury to Cup
semi-final in mid sixties.
Now believed to be a
prison officer at
Wakefield.

captained the Kangaroos from full-back while in front of him were Noel Pidding, Harry Wells, a big, strong punishing tackler, Alex Watson, even bigger than Wells, and speed merchant Ian Moir. At half-back were crafty Keith Holman, now a top-class referee, and Ken McCaffery, one of the most versatile players in Australia. The forwards were all powerful. Roy Bull, balding but good; hooker Ken Kearney, who knew all about English methods, having played for Leeds in many matches; Duncan Hall, the best prop forward I ever saw play for Australia, Norm "Sticks" Provan, tall and lanky and partnered in the second row by fearless Brian "Bull" Davies. The loose forward was Peter Diversi, ideally built for a lock, as he would be called in Australia.

"What can our 'unknowns' do against this lot but collapse?" said one official in the train going down to Lyons.

What they did was win.

The pace of this conflict was set in the first half with an incident that portrayed Britain's guts. Twenty-year-old international newcomer Mick Sullivan took a pass in the centre and met Harry Wells' solid 15 stones in frontal impact. He went down under the crash and when I saw him stagger to his feet with a gash in his left eye I thought it must be the end of him and Britain's hopes. He left the field and Dave Valentine went on stand-off half, Australia realising this was the time to start punishing Britain's defence.

The "Lions" were leading by 7 points to 5 as the Australians swarmed round their twenty-five yards line, then Valentine went away on the left wing to beat Moir and turn the ball inside to lively Frank Kitchen from Leigh. Kitch went zig-zagging across the field looking for wide-open spaces, his speed taking him round Churchill and Wells to score with a yard to spare from the out-of-bounds line. Three points. Up came Jimmie Ledgard to take the difficult kick and as it went over the voices of Britain sounded loudly. They were even louder a few seconds later when Mick Sullivan came back wearing an eye plaster and ear-caps to give him protection.

The Lions hadn't finished yet and when Gordon Brown from Leeds ran in two quick tries the Australians were baffled and bewildered and defeated. They lost Duncan Hall, their tough forward, and only when Britain relaxed in the late stages of the game did they add a few points to their score, making it 13 to Britain's 28. Gordon Brown and Phil Jackson scored two tries each for Britain with David Rose and Kitchen one apiece. Ledgard, who later kicked his record 100th goal of the season, hit home five good ones. For Australia, Harry Wells, two, and Kearney scored tries while Noel Pidding kicked two goals.

It was a happy British party who drank champagne in a Lyons *bistro* that night, a special toast being given to the fighting Sullivan.

After a week's rest Britain went further South to meet France at Toulouse, where a crowd of close on 40,000 saw two unbeaten teams face up to each other. The only changes in the Lions' team were Ally Naughton coming in at centre and Mick Sullivan moving to the wing to replace Kitchen.

It was an amazingly fast game and full of rip-roaring rugby. It looked as though Britain might win when Helme made a dummying run and scored the try of the match, but in the dying stages French winger Contrastin dived over for fine try to make it 13–13. It all depended on Puig Aubert's kick, and he missed, leaving the scores level.

While Britain were holding France, the Australians were in Marseilles playing the Kiwis. They galloped to an early lead after a good first try by Watson and picked up 16 points before New Zealand could get back in the game. With Clive Churchill starring, Australia ran out winners with 34 points to 15. The Kiwis had to go to Bordeaux the following Thursday knowing that Britain would pull out all the stops for a victory to make sure either of winning the tournament or at the worst being equal with France.

The Kiwis startled Britain by taking control and the lead with goals by McKay. Not until ten minutes from the interval did Britain manage to settle down, tries being scored by Kitchen, Rose and Brown for an 11–6 lead. Not big enough to relax, for the Kiwi forwards with Big Bill McLellan in charge had really worried the British.

The pattern changed in the second half when a revived Lions struck hard and often. Led by Helme from the scrum base their backs scintillated. Phil Jackson, now a coach in N.S.W., began the scoring with a great side-stepping try and then Frank Kitchen, back in the team as left-winger, with Sullivan moved back to the centre, also went over. Unfortunately, Kitchen still had leg trouble which had not cleared from the Australian match and didn't see out the game.

Britain's success was crowned in the late stages when Ledgard linked up with his backs to score a fine try to add to his four goals. Kitche, two, Brown, Rose, Jackson and Ledgard shared the six trirs. New Zealand could score only six points with three McKay goals to Britain's 26. The Lions were now certain of a place in the Final.

France had to beat Australia to tie with Britain for a play-off, which they did at Nantes, 15–3. Thus the final placings were Britain and France 5 points each, with Australia 2 and New Zealand showing nothing for their 12,000 miles journey.

Jimmy Ledgard kicking
for goal during the 1954
World Cup campaign in
France. Ledgard is an
all-time favourite.

Now we had a Great Britain *v* France play-off to look
forward to.

As I walked into the Parc du Prince Stadium in Paris
on November 13th, I remembered what an airport official
had said three weeks earlier as he watched the party
board the plane: "That lot are wasting their time." Some-
how I thought he'd have to eat his words even more than
he had done already, though Kitchen was still unfit,
Naughton being recalled to centre and Sullivan moved
back to wing.

Jim Ledgard was not on his best goal-kicking form and
missed an early chance. Not so Puig Aubert, who kicked
a superb goal after 11 minutes and sent the French crowd
roaring his nick-name *"Pipette! Pipette!"* Then David

Rose, the Scot from Hawick, scored Britain's first try, running round Cantoni cleverly. The middle men of Britain's backs were their strength and Gordon Brown scored, to create a record along with Rose of a try in each of the four games. Britain had a four-point lead at half time but it wasn't sufficient, five points by the French soon following after resumption. Then Puig Aubert added a goal and Britain were in real trouble. Valentine led his forwards well and the experience gained in English Cup football meant much in this dangerous spell. It was the dazzling Helme who restored Britain's lead. He went side-stepping under the posts and this time Ledgard made sure with the extra two points. He did even better when he sent Brown away down the short

French forward Henri Lacaze attempts to fend off a tackle from Australian Rex Mossop in the 1960 World Cup encounter at Wigan. Mossop is now a well-known Rugby League television commentator in Sydney, Australia.

side to score in the corner. A 16 points to 9 lead looked safe but worry came again when Contrastin scored, drawing forth whistles of delight from the French. The most welcome whistle of all came when the referee signalled the end of the match.

A small band of English supporters shouldered veterans Helme and Valentine off the field for the Cup presentation. A great moment for all of us.

After Britain's unexpected success in the first World Cup with a makeshift side, the second competition of 1957, staged in Australia, looked like being a walk-over for us. A strong, experienced squad was selected in Moses, Boston, Jackson, Jones, Sullivan, Price, Stevenson, Prescott, Harris, Little, Grundy, Gunney and Turner, with Rhodes, Whiteley, Ashton, McKinney, Davies regarded as the reserves. Note the name of Eric Ashton on the Australian scene for the first time. He was to grace the name of British Rugby League for many years.

I had incurred the wrath of some Australian fans by writing that it was hardly worth paying the cost of the big trophy by taking it to Sydney. It should be so easy for Britain to win with a side like this against the sort of team Australia could field.

But the tournament collapsed badly for Britain. An extra game was played on the way out, in Perth, and stand-off half Ray Price was injured, which proved disastrous. I always felt it was a mistake to play this match. Britain started well by beating France and when Australia beat New Zealand it was pretty obvious that the Australia *v* Great Britain game would provide the winners. Injuries handicapped Britain during the match, which Australia won 30–6, the six points coming from the boot of Lewis Jones to virtually close, far too soon, his big-match career. Jones was blamed in some quarters for Britain's flop. That can only be opinion; what is certain is that many people thought as I did that there was still a lot of big football in him. Australia had a clean sweep in this World Cup and Britain slumped worse when they lost to New Zealand. The Kangaroos had gained their revenge for that unexpected 1954 defeat. The big Cup stayed in Sydney.

*Opposite:* England versus France, 1980. David Ward is halted.

The 1960 World Cup series in Britain was full of incident and, not surprisingly, the decider between the Lions and Australia one of the most hotly-contested games ever seen on these shores.

Great Britain fielded Austin Rhodes (St. Helens), Billy Boston (Wigan), Eric Ashton (Wigan), Alan Davies (Oldham), Mick Sullivan (Wigan), Frank Myler (Widnes), and Alex Murphy (St. Helens), Jack Wilkinson (Wakefield) John Shaw (Halifax), Brian McTigue (Wigan), Derek Turner (Wakefield) Brian Shaw (Hunslet) and Vince Karalius (St. Helens). What a pack of forwards!

Australia played Keith Barnes, Ron Boden, Reg Gasnier, Harry Wells, Brian Carlson, Barry Muir and Tony Brown, Dub Beattie, Noel Kelly, Bernie Purcell, Rex Mossop, Elton Rasmussen and Brian Hambley. John Raper, their best lock forward for years, was out of action.

Austin Rhodes was the British kicker and his first goal after a few misses was a beauty. Two points to nil after seven minutes. Britain were getting the ball from the scrum but being kicked down as soon as they had it. Then things began to happen. Purcell had words from the referee for a vigorous tackle, Reg Gasnier just man-

One of Australia's best ever stand off halves Bobby Fulton is well held by French prop Francis De Nadi during a 1970 World Cup match at Bradford.

aged to avoid a stiff arm, Sullivan was flattened on the touchline and seven forwards had a flare-up. But Britain weren't put out of their stride and the risk taken in playing Boston paid dividends when the 15-stone winger from Wigan used every ounce of his strength to score in the corner, Rhodes kicking another gem from the touchline. Mick Sullivan came back to the fray to finish off an effort by Karalius while Murphy added another 3 points to give Britain a ten-point lead. The mud was taking its toll and the margin was more than welcome.

Tempers didn't improve in the heavy conditions and flare-ups continued periodically during the game, the referee having a hard job to keep control. He did not send anyone, off though many might have gone.

Ten minutes from time Australia got a consolation try from winger Carlson after a long run by Tony Brown. A brave kick by Barnes was just short and Australia had lost their chance. The mud was the winner in a match where the best players, like Gasnier for instance, were never seen.

Never one of the most popular competitions with Rugby League officialdom, the world tournament was put into cold storage until 1968 when the match venues were shared between both Australia and New Zealand. And its place in the British popularity chart nose-dived further when they crashed to a 25 points to 10 defeat at the hands of the old enemy Australia in Sydney.

The handling of the match by New Zealand referee John Percival was certainly not appreciated by the British and his application of the laws against the Poms saw Australian full-back Eric Simms kick eight goals. Worse still, holders Great Britain effectively crashed out of the tournament when they were beaten 7–2 by France in the clinging mud of Carlaw Park, Auckland. The British did win one match in the series, crushing New Zealand 38 points to 14, but the bitterness of having lost their title without having played in the final was not easily accepted by the disappointed Pom party. In the final the Australians took the title comfortably beating France 20 points to two in front of an ecstatic Sydney crowd of 54,290.

Australia's 1970 World
Cup squad.

Two years later, 1970, on home territory the British attempted to regain their lost crown. The squad, led by experienced captain Frank Myler of St Helens, who had just inspired a Ashes win in Australia, was full of confidence.

Those buoyant hopes were fuelled when the British boys topped the qualifying League table after three credi-table wins, including an 11 points to four triumph over the champions Australia at Leeds. But Australia were reluctant to hand over their title to the Poms and the final at Headingley on 7th November proved to be their day.

The British, who had been the best footballing side in the competition prior to the final, seemed determined to knock the Aussies back down-under with physical aggression and they tossed their matching-winning style right out of the window. The Australians were more than delighted with their 12 points to seven victory and all their bruises mattered little with the trophy still in their hands.

And so, another two years later in 1972, this time across the English Channel in France, the scene was set for yet another world series clash between the giants, Great Britain and Australia. Again the British made all the early running beating the Aussies 27 points to 21 in their qualifying encounter at Perpignan.

As in the previous series Great Britain topped the qualifying League and Australia finished second, having beaten both France and New Zealand. With France eliminated from the tournament the French rugby public deserted the competition and a pitiful number of 4,500 turned up for the final at Lyons on 11th November. They were to be the privileged few because the match turned out to be a Rugby League classic.

Much-travelled forward Terry Clawson, then playing with Leeds, gave Great Britain an early lead with an angled penalty, but the Australians fought back to overtake the British. Prop John O'Neill forced 30 yards on his own for a touch-down, which winger Ray Branighan goaled.

The Australians controlled the game, but they could not break down a gritty British defence. That failure was thrown back in their faces when British winger and captain Clive Sullivan ran 80 yards from deep inside his own half to score a spectacular, solo try.

That try has flashed across British television screens many times as a classic of its kind and it never fails to excite me even today.

Early in the second half Australia regained the lead. Artie Beetson, one of the finest footballing forwards ever to wear the Australian green and gold, bounced over for a try and Branighan hit the target with his goal kick.

Again the British rolled up their sleeves and Sullivan who lit the flame. After creating a gap in the Australian defence he put second row forward Brian Lockwood (Castleford) clear. An intelligent piece of supporting play by Dewsbury hooker Mick Stephenson – he was later to be a very successful export to Sydney Rugy League – and Britain had their second try.

Clawson booted over the goal and that had the scores tied at 10 points each. Extra time of 10 minutes each way was played, but, as there was no further score, Britain took the title by virtue of scoring the most points in the qualifying matches. Revenge was sweet for the gallant Poms!

In a brave attempt to find an acceptable formula for the competition, the international administrators decided to try a new format for the 1975 series. Instead of staging the tournament based in either the northern or southern hemispheres it was split into three sections. The first stage was devoted entirely to domestic competition with England, France and a revitalised Welsh team forming one part and Australia and New Zealand the other.

The second stage took the European contingent down-under while the third was staged in Europe. The formula never really caught on with any of the nation's paying customers and the biggest gate was for the points each draw between Australia and England in Sydney when 33,858 saw the game. England beat Australia 16 points to 13 at Wigan in the closing stages but England's chances of winning the title were ruined by an unexpected defeat by Wales 12 points to seven in Brisbane. Australia took the title when the final table was worked out.

Following that attempt to widen the scope of the competition, the International Board decided to abandon the World Championship as a concept and return to nations crossing the world for extended tours. And there have been no signs that this system will be changed despite the arrival of Papua New Guinea as full members of the Board.

# 6

# THE AUSTRALIAN TESTS

How much the Rugby League countries owe to a young man named A. H. Baskerville no one will ever know. In 1907 this 25-year-old New Zealander heard about the game in England and gathered a team of footballers around him to look at a rule book he had received. With no guarantees either of money or matches, they called in at Sydney on their way to Britain and persuaded "Dally" Messenger, Australia's greatest player, to join their proposed tour. As a result of this visit the N.S.W. Rugby League was formed and young Baskerville left triumphantly for home, only to be tragically struck down en route. He was taken ill in Brisbane and died. What a pioneering spirit the boy had and what a lead he gave Rugby League football!

As a result of Baskerville's enterprise the first official Test took place in London on December 12th, 1908, two others being played in Newcastle and Birmingham. England won two with one drawn, 22 points each.

Messenger captained the Australian team in the first two Tests and played well. I never saw him in action but I did see him kick off in a country match in Queensland many years later. As he did so his shoe came off and travelled as far as the ball. From that moment I have never agreed to V.I.P.'s kicking off at all. Late in life, Messenger was helped by the Australian Board of Control and lived at the palatial eight-storey club in Phillip Street, Sydney, owned by the N.S.W. Rugby League. Australia is one of the countries where they look after and cherish their famed footballers.

In that first Test here Billy Batten scored two tries for

England while Jimmy Deveraux, who later came to play for Hull, had three and Messenger kicked five goals for Australia.

A word about Billy Batten. He was a wing-three-quarter who played with Hunslet and later moved, for a record £600, to Hull where he became a legendary figure. Big, beetle-browed, black-haired Batten is recognised as the greatest centre, next to Wagstaff, who ever played for England.

Strong and fearless, Billy would gallop down the field in the black and white irregular stripes of Hull with his knees high, a player known and feared yet liked by everyone. He it was who introduced the leap-over-an-opponent trick, not readily accepted now by referees and rarely seen. The story is told of Batten's clash with a famous New Zealand player called Opai Asher. Both were pretty good jumpers and when they opposed each other in one match they took off together, meeting in mid-air. I'm told it was Asher who was taken to hospital.

Batten began his international career in 1908–9 against the Australians and ended it in 1921, happily in a match at Hull. In his prime he was the highest-paid footballer in Rugby League, his wage at Hull being £14 a match, equivalent to £150 these days. For Cup games he received more, of course. A lot of his money was given away: in the depression days after the First World War he didn't forget his old friends in his native Yorkshire village of Hemsforth and also often made sure folk in neighbouring villages weren't without food.

Billy, whose son Eric followed in his footsteps and wore his country's colours against Australia, died a few years ago after a long illness. His name will never be forgotten in Rugby League circles, particularly on Humberside where he made his name a household word.

On the first tour of Australia in 1910 (tours take place in alternate countries every four years) only two official Test matches were played and England won them both. On the Agricultural Show ground in Sydney they won by 27 points to 20 and on the Brisbane Exhibition ground they had a five-point margin, 22–17.

Jimmy Lomas captained and played centre in both

*Opposite:* Steve Rogers one of Australia's finest ever centre three quarters carries the ball against Great Britain.

Tom Raudonikis

Graham Eadie

Michael Cronin

Tests and Jimmy Leytham, the right winger, had six tries in the two games. Forward Jukes got three in the first Test.

The success of this tour encouraged Australia to return to England quickly and in November 1911 they played at Newcastle. In the mid-thirties an effort was made to maintain a Rugby League club in Newcastle and they played for a season or so in the Northern Rugby League. One or two good players like winger J. Williamson, who went to Wigan, and Stan Edwards were found, but the strength of soccer in the north-east proved too much and the club folded up.

Australia won the Ashes in 1911, being undefeated in the three Tests at Newcastle, Edinburgh and Birmingham. The Scottish Test was drawn, 11–11. All the Australian players on the tour came from N.S.W. and included Billy Cann, who has served Australian R.L. for over half a century. Billy had toured with the Pioneers and also on the 1908 tour. He tells the story of passing through Liverpool's Lime Street station when Jack Fihelly, who later became Minister of Queensland Railways, tossed a florin into a blind man's hat. The coin fell to the ground, and a team-mate, Dan Frawley, dived for it, beaten only by the blind man!

On the 1911 tour, Cann had a relative with him called Steve Darmody, who later returned to make his home in

Hull. He told how Darmody in one match was having a lot of trouble in the scrum. Darmody said someone was putting a hand over his eyes and he couldn't see the ball coming in. "I told him," said Cann "that it was easy – just bite his fingers the next time the hand comes over."

"In the next scrum I saw the hand come over myself and went to grab it," said Billy, "but Steve's teeth moved faster and he fastened them round a finger all right – mine! I nearly lost my thumb!" Cann had the mark for years.

When the 1908 team arrived, someone asked a forward what he thought of London. "It's a great place," he said, "but crikey, ain't there a lot of pommies about."

Harold Wagstaff got his first try, two in fact, for England against the Australians in Edinburgh in December 1911, which enabled England to draw 11–11. The referee was a character who became famous for his knickerbocker trousers and drooping moustache, Frank Renton of Hunslet. Mr. Renton once chased a player who was chasing another to kick him in the rear. Renton was so fast that he arrived at the same time as the kicker did and waited before the boot was raised, but with Renton looking on it never landed.

Stand-off Chris McKivatt was the Australian captain and a great leader. He had the honour and thrill of scoring two tries on New Year's Day, 1912, which made sure the Kangaroos took the Ashes back to Australia. The Australian full-back on that tour was Howard Hallet, whom Australian followers of the old school consider their best-ever. If he were better than Clive Churchill he must have been very good.

Jimmy Lomas scored a try for England on that New Year's Day defeat of 33 points to 8 and ended his career in the red, white and blue jersey.

In 1914, England went in search of the Ashes and brought them back before war was declared. Harold Wagstaff led England in Sydney and won the first Test handsomely by 23 points to 5. For the first time a Queenslander, H. Bowleski, was in the Australian Test team; he kicked a goal. Stanley Moorhouse, Wagstaff's club wing partner from Huddersfield, got two tries with another Fartowner, wrestling champion Douglas Clarke, getting a try. Australia kept in the series by taking the second Test on the Sydney cricket ground by 12 points to 7. Frank Burge, scored in this game. He was among Australia's greatest ever forwards.

Then came the "Rorke's Drift" Test in which England finished with nine fit men but won the match and the Ashes, probably their finest win of all time. Oldham full-back A. E. Wood kicked four goals to make the difference of the two tries each side scored: 14 points to 6 and the Ashes were back in England, with tours over until the end of the war.

When tours were resumed six years later Britain went to Australia but lost the Ashes by two games to one. Harold Wagstaff went as captain but did not play in the third Test, which England won. The closest match was the first, won by Australia 8 points to 4, Ben Gronow kicking both goals. Harold Horder, Australia's best-ever

Australian Tourists 1959.

winger, was in his first Test and kicked a goal to add to tries by Frank Burge and C. ("Chuck") Fraser. Australia made sure of the series when they won easily by 21 points to 8. Frank Gallagher and "Chick" Johnson got England's two tries but five tries to Australia through Potter, Farnsworth, Horder, Vest and Gilbert put paid to England.

There was some consolation when Britain saved the tour from being a clean Australian sweep by winning 23–13. Herman Hilton, two, Billy Stone, two, and Jim Bacon shared five tries, with Johnny Rogers kicking three and Square Stockwell two goals. Normally at scrum half, Rogers was on the wing. The two wingers were goal-kickers – how often does that happen I wonder? A year later Australia were back in England for the first time for ten years.

October 1921, and one point at Headingley won the first Test for England, 6–5. Referee was veteran Frank Renton, the man in the knee-covered breeches. Stockwell, the Leeds winger, scored the late vital try after Cecil Blinkhorn had gone over for the Kangaroos and Jimmy Craig had kicked a goal. Australia, for whom Sid Pearce and Frank Burge were in a strong pack, were disappointed at the close result.

At Hull, a reasonably happy hunting ground for the Kangaroos, they had a fairly easy passage for the second Test and won by 16 points to 2. Billy Batten was back in Test football and Jonty Parkin captained Britain, but the famous Australian wing pair, Horder and Blinkhorn, had three tries to add to one by Dick Vest. Duncan Thompson, the scrum half, kicked two goals and it was the third Test which decided the series at Salford in the mid-January mud of 1922. A close game, 6–0, it was won by us through Hilton and Gallagher tries. The Ashes were back in England.

The first time the name J. Sullivan appeared on the Test scene was in 1924. What a nuisance he was to be for the Australians! On the Sydney cricket ground in his first Test he kicked five goals, England winning 22–3; Johnny Ring, Wigan's flying Welsh winger, didn't score but was in the picture to help Jonty Parkin score two tries. Sid Rix and Jack Price scored one each. Tommy Gorman was in the Australian side, Horder was still there and so was Ces Aynsley, later to come to Rochdale in Lancashire.

Barrow, the outpost of English Rugby League, had sent Charlie Carr and Bill Burgess in the successful 1924 team. England made no mistake with the second Test but it was only a Sullivan goal which made the difference. An Aynsley try for Australia was cancelled out with a Parkin try. This was the game when Frank Gallagher played at stand-off and the Sydney crowd thought he was a push-over.

Australia made sure there was no three-win clean sweep – there never has been, although the 1962 series came very close – and Britain went down 21–11. Parkin got his usual try, Frank Evans from Swinton got two and Sullivan kicked a goal.

Australia did not return the visit to England because of the New Zealand tour of 1926 and England went back in 1928. Sullivan, made captain, kicked three goals in the first Test at Brisbane, where Tommy Gorman was being groomed as Australian captain, an honour granted him in 1929. The St. Helens pair, Les Fairclough and Alfred Ellaby, got their first Test tries along with Wakefield's Big Bill Horton. When England won the second Test of this tour on the cricket ground at Sydney the clean sweep was again possible. It isn't often an international side is nilled, but for the first time Australia did not score. Parkin was back as skipper and got his try along with one by Ellaby and a goal by Sullivan for an 8–0 victory. But Australia came back in the third game to win 21–14, despite two Fairclough tries and four Sullivan goals. The name of Benny Wearing was in the Australian records for the first time. He got two tries and three goals in this match.

Probably one of the best-ever captains Australia had was Tommy Gorman, who brought the 1929 side to England. This was a tour which had many games schedules; things have altered since then because officials don't want players to miss "home" games. That goes for both countries. Gorman's men played 35 matches, won 24 lost

9 and drew 2. They scored 708 points to 347 but lost the Ashes.

Leading points-scorer was Eric Weissel, a stand-off of exceptional ability, followed by the man who later came to England. Big Bill Shankland, who had his century points. Two fast wingers were Alan Ridley and Bill Spencer, both from the bush country, while Cecil Fifield and Joe Busch, who later returned to play at Hull and Leeds, were also in a side of more than average ability. Vic Ambruster, who later signed for Rochdale, was in the forwards along with George Bishop, later a Test referee, and Wally Prigg, who became an Australian captain, as loose forward.

The first Test match was a disaster for Britain, who lost 31 points to 8 at Hull. It was the only Test for which Jim Sullivan was dropped, and he was recalled along with Jonty Parkin for the second and third Tests at Leeds and Swinton, When the third game proved scoreless a replay was requested and granted after persuasion by Harry Sunderland, the volatile Australian manager. The replay at Rochdale, with two youngsters in the three-quarter line – Stan Brogden and Stan Smihh – resulted in a British win by a solitary Smith try scored on the touchline side. Peculiarly, we were down on the scores aggregate by 34 points to 30. Yet this has often happened although Britain has more Test wins.

The 1929 Australian side certainly had many remarkably good footballers in their party, starting with Frank McMillan at full-back right down to Herb Steinhort in the forwards. Australia's try by Chimpy Busch in the Swinton Test, in which a touch judge said "No", lost them the Ashes. No doubt it did. The very fair-minded Bill Shankland always claimed it was a try. But the record book says Britain won the Ashes in the only tour in which four Tests were played.

After the sensational 1929 tour Britain won the 1932 series by the usual number of two games to one. This time it was the second Test which Australia won. The first in Sydney had gone to the Lions by 8 points to 6. Big "Bruss" Atkinson from Castleford was in his first Test in Australia and scored a try along with Ellaby, who later became a resident of Castleford and a director of the club. Stan Brogden, whom Australians reckoned was the fastest Englishman they ever saw on an Australian ground, was in the centre as partner to Stan Smith, the man who had won the fourth Test in 1929.

A tough match in Brisbane swung the game in favour of Australia. They are all tough matches in Australia but this was particularly so. Hec Gee, who in 1945 I signed from Wigan for Leeds, was scrum half for Australia. He got a couple of tries along with one by Joe Wilson, who also joined Wigan. Tom Brown, a Wigan director, was on tour as a visitor with the English party and when he wasn't playing his fiddle for the amusement of the team he was checking on players – Australians. He managed to persuade Gee and Wilson that Wigan in Lancashire had more to offer than Ipswich, Queensland. Gee came and stayed, Wilson came, moved to Bradford for a spell then returned home. Stan Smith and Ernest Pollard got English tries but it wasn't sufficient and it was a third decider in Sydney.

Britain won by 18 points to 13 with the left-winger partnership of Brogden and Smith doing the damage and sharing the tries, three to Smith and one to "Broggy". Sullivan kicked goals but for once was out-kicked by Eric Weissel, who with more chances accounted for five goals. A terrific English pack of Joe Thompson, Les White, Albert Fildes, Martin Hodgson, Nat Silcock and Bill Horton must have been a sight for its size alone. All big 'uns. Though in the opposition Mick Steinhort, Frank O'Connor and Sid Pearce were not small lads.

Australia came back to England just over a year later and played the first Test at Belle Vue, Manchester. Two Sullivan goals did the necessary and for the second time Australia were nilled. Dave Brown, a prolific points scorer for Australia, was on this tour and liked England so much that he later came back to play for Warrington. Brown, completely bald and wearing ear-caps, was a terrific goal kicker and is still with the Australian Rugby League as a coach and schoolboy association promoter. He coached the South African touring side who went to Australia and had much to do with the American "All-

Stars" who also toured Australia. What he could not do in the first Test in 1933 he did in the second Test at Leeds, scoring a try and kicking a goal, but it wasn't sufficient, for Sullivan kicked two goals which, with a Wood try, gave Britain victory and the Ashes. Gus Risman was now on the international scene and so were fellow-Salfordians Barney Hudson and Jack Feetham.

Britain made it a clean sweep at Swinton, if only by a short head of one try; Sullivan kicked five goals, so did Dave Brown. Hudson, Feetham and Smith scored the three tries to the two by Vic Hey and Wally Prigg. The name of Ray Stehr appeared in this series for the first time and we were to see and hear much of him before the 'thirties were out.

Dave Brown returned to Australia to lead the Kangaroos in the next home series in 1936 and to win the first Test by 24 points to 8 for the Lions. Arthur Atkinson captained the side in place of the elected captain, Jim Brough, in the first Test. Alan Edwards and Harry Beverly scored tries, but the redoubtable Don Bradman of Australian Rugby League, Dave Brown, scored two and kicked four goals in their convincing win. Up in sunny Queensland, England squared the series when Edwards got two tries and Risman kicked two goals with one by Martin Hodgson to gain a 12–7 win.

The decider came in mid-July, 1936, with the power pack of England in Silcock, Armitt, Woods, Arkwright, Hodgson and Beverly. The game became rough and Stehr and Arkwright finished earlier than the others, taking marching orders. Risman captained the side in place of Brough and with Barney Hudson, one try, and Stan Brogden, one, plus three goals by that long kicker Martin Hodgson, Britain kept Australia down to a Vic Hey try and two goals by Dave Brown. It was a thrilling series.

The last tour before the Second World War came in 1937. In the first Test Australia once again ended with a point on the wrong side for them at Headingley, Leeds. Although Beaton had two goals for Australia, we scored the only try through Emlyn Jenkins and a goal by Hodgson gave England the first and vital Test win. Risman was captain and newcomers to the scene were Castleford's centre Jim Croston and winger Bernard Cunniffee. The second Test was an easier win, with Alan Edwards back on the left wing and two tries to show for his return. His club partner Barney Hudson had replaced Wigan's Jack Morley, and with Watkins and Jenkins the halves it was a pretty good Salford contribution. And the whole 13 points were shared by "Reds" with Edwards, Hudson and Risman.

This wasn't by any means the best Australian side sent over, but they took the third Test at Huddersfield with Jack Reardon, now the R.L. writer on the *Courier Mail* up in Brisbane, getting one of three tries; Herb Narvo and Andy Norval scored the other two and Jack Beaton had two goals. The only English try was scored by Barney Hudson.

The tours for another nine years were over. War had come once again.

In 1946 I was one of the first three journalists to tour Australia with the Lions.

Under the captaincy of Gus Risman the party sailed in the aircraft carrier *Indomitable*, a name by which the team were to be known. It was a great side and the first team to be undefeated in a three-match Test series in Australia: two wins and a draw of 8 points each. In the first Test, Jack Kitching of Bradford was sent off for "striking" after he alleged he had been bitten. He had too, for I saw the teeth marks myself! The scorers for Australia were Lionel Cooper, who later came to Huddersfield, and Ron Bailey who had returned to Sydney after playing with Huddersfield.

This first post-War tour did a great deal to put Australian and English football back on its international feet.

The Kangaroos came to England in 1948. I had persuaded the Australians to disembark at Marseilles in France and flew over in a charter plane on behalf of the Huddersfield club to bring the tourists to play their first game at Fartown. My idea was a success and the tour opened dramatically before a big gate, over 26,000 in an all-ticket match. Dramatically because Johnny "Whacker" Graves was involved in an incident with Johnny Hunter, Huddersfield's Australian full-back. It was a tough, hard match and the shape of things to come.

The recently-arrived Australians lost by 26 points to 3, but they quickly found their land legs and by the end of the tour had won 15 games and lost 12. Two matches were abandoned because of fog, including the third Test which was later played when the tourists came back from France. Played at Bradford's Odsal Stadium, this became known as the "Battle of Britain".

Colin Maxwell was the captain and Bill Tyquin vice-captain of the 1948 party. This was the touring side which brought 28 players instead of the usual 26, including an extra hooker and scrum half. Jack Raynor, a policeman who collected British truncheons as souvenirs, had the most appearances with 19 matches in England. Horrigan had most tries with 13 and Graves most goals, 24. Several mayors from different towns kicked off on the tour, which brought the comment from Australian "Dutchy" Holland. "These 'Pommies' will do anything to get a scrum." (A scrum had to be formed after a V.I.P. had kicked off and Holland knew that usually British teams dominated the pack and set scrums).

Nineteen forty-eight was the year of big gates in sport-starved Britain. All three Tests were won in each case with record receipts. At Leeds, 36,529 paid £8,020, at Swinton, 37,137 parted with £6,764, while the third Test at Odsal attracted 43,500 and £6,877.

The second post-War tour to Australia in 1950 was under the captaincy of Ernest Ward, a Dewsbury-reared centre-threequarter who signed for Bradford Northern at the age of sixteen, a signing which caused a storm of trouble at Dewsbury. Ward was a natural footballer and his side a good one. So much so that the party had visions of going through the tour undefeated. Wigan had created a record by sending seven players and then made it eight when Les Williams (Hunslet) withdrew and Gordon Ratcliffe took his place.

The first test was won gallantly by Britain 6–4 in thick mud on the Sydney cricket ground, Jack Hilton, now a Wigan director, scoring both our tries against two goals by Noel Pidding. The Queensland part of the tour started well with a big score of 88 points to nil against Central Queensland, but then trouble started. Referee rows and other problems brought defeat in the second Test at Brisbane (3–15), which was followed by another win for Australia on an even worse mud-covered Sydney ground by 5–2, giving them the Ashes after being many years without them. Australians went mad with delight, scooping up the mud and licking it. "We thought we'd never do it," they said.

Aussie Skipper Clive Churchill, christened "The Little Master" (after Dally Messenger, "The Master"). played a great game and was carried off shoulder-high. There were record receipts from 19 games, four of which the Lions lost, including the two Tests.

The 1952 Kangaroos had a good side, losing only three matches out of 27 played. They had Clive Churchill at his best at full-back, good backs in Harry Wells, Ken McCaffery, Noel Pidding, Brian Carlson, Keith Holman and Frank Stanmore, and tough forwards in Duncan Hall, Roy Bull, C. Collinson, Ken Kearney and Brian Davies.

They started the tour well but fell in the first Test at Headingley, where Barrow boys Frank Castle, Ted Toohey and Willie Horne shone. A great try by Castle, the R.U. man from the Midlands, and five goals by the master of side-foot goal-kicking. Willie Horne, gave Britain a win by 19 points to 6.

The Kangaroos tore into the club sides with remarkable football force and gained many great victories. But again the big moment proved too much, for in the second Test at Swinton Britain won by 21 points to 5. Ernest Ward led the side well with a try and two goals, added to tries by Castle and Doug Greeball, two each, and a dropped goal by Horne. There was some consolation for the Kangaroos, who continued to win the county and club games with ease. The tourists at last showed their true form in the third Test at Bradford and won by 27 points to 7. Noel Pidding kicked six goals while Holman and Stanmore were the stars at half back. The tourists went to France wondering how they could play such good football yet lose the Ashes. They had the best scoring record of any touring side to this country – 816 points against 248.

Four years later Britain had coaching problems and lost the first Test. The series was squared up in Brisbane when Lewis Jones kicked ten goals, one more than Pidding had kicked in the first Test, and it all rested on the final Sydney game, which the Lions lost 16–20, British players claiming that a deciding try by centre Harry Wells should not have been awarded. They considered he had grounded the ball the wrong side of the line before he went over.

This was the tour when the New South Wales v Great Britain match was abandoned after an outburst of rough play; the referee said he could not control the players and walked off. It was the first time such a thing had happened and the British players later apologised to the Australian Board of Control.

Two years later, in 1956, the Kangaroos tour open the Test series at Wigan. Ian Moir, a flying winger, scored first but before the end Britain had won by 21 points to 10. Billy Boston, before his own folk, scored two typical tries with Alan Davies, Mick Sullivan and Jack Grundy getting the others. Wakefield's Frank Mortimer, in his first Test match, kicked three goals.

Australia reshuffled their team for the second Test and won by almost the same score as Britain did the first, but this time it was 22 points to Britain's 9. The Odsal ground was heavy, so were the British players, and that lively Aussie scrum half Keith Holman, scored a try along with Banks, Bull and Davies; full-back Clifford kicked five goals. Jeff Stevenson, who never toured Australia apart from the 1957 World Cup, scored Britain's only try. Team changes gave Britain a better chance for the Ashes, which they took at Swinton by nilling the Kangaroos and scoring 19 points. It was the first time since 1930 that the Kangaroos had been nilled in England. But they were rebuilding their team, as later efforts showed.

In 1958 the British touring team had their hands full, for Australia were by then world champions, having taken the 1957 World Cup in Sydney. Alan Prescott led

Australian Touring Team 1959. Second Test – Headingley November 1959. N. Fox scores a try for Great Britain.

the party and for the first time a coach was taken in Jim Brough, a former tour captain. This was an amazing tour for out of 21 matches played Britain lost only one, the first Test 8–25, while one was drawn.

In the first half of the second Test in Brisbane, British skipper Alan Prescott broke his arm in a midfield collision and if he had gone off I think Australia would have won, and taken the Ashes too, for Britain had already lost stand-off half David Bolton with a broken collarbone. But Prescott gallantly stayed on and although the team's doctor told him not to return to the field after the interval he insisted on doing so. Unable to tackle, he directed his depleted side to one of the greatest-ever Test victories: 25–18.

The third Test, in Sydney, was an astonishing affair, Queensland referee Mr. Casey being bombarded with oranges, apples and bottles after allowing advantage at an obstruction. Britain won by the record score of 40 points to 17, Mick Sullivan playing brilliantly. He set up a new try record on this tour with 38. Eric Fraser kicked 110 goals and we scored a record points tally of 810 against 378.

In 1959 (out of cycle because of the World Cup), a Welshman, Keith Barnes, who had emigrated to Australia, led the Kangaroos on their tour of 24 matches, of which 15 were won and 9 lost. They were outsiders in the Tests but won the first at Swinton with a real shock and a score of 22 points to 14. Reg Gasnier, making his Test debut in this country, was the man of the match and scored three tries, helped a great deal by that strong, tough centre "Dealer" Wells, who also got a try. Keith Barnes had five goals. Billy Boston and Derek Turner scored Britain's two tries and Eric Fraser kicked four goals.

Britain's luck turned and the Ashes were saved when a one-point victory, 11–10, put the series equal at Leeds. The Australians will always say that a scrum given under the posts from which Johnny Whiteley scored a try from a Stevenson pass should not have been awarded.

The third Test at Wigan belonged to Neil Fox, who scored 15 of Britain's 18 points. His six goals to the three by Barnes were the difference, for two tries were scored by Southward and Fox for Britain and by Raper and Carlson for Australia. Gasnier did not score but he ran on a heavy Central Park ground in such a way that he engineered the highlight of the match. He ran from near his own posts on a super gallop, slipping tackles, giving a dummy and finally sending a pass to Carlson for the winger to score. A wonderful memory.

When Great Britain toured Australia and New Zealand in 1962, they came within two points of being the only team to win all three Tests in Australia. Eric Ashton was the captain and after taking the first Test easily by 31 points to 12 in Sydney and the second 17–10 at Brisbane, the scene was set for a clean sweep. But they lost two men when Mick Sullivan and Derek Turner were sent off. Australia's Beatty was also dismissed.

Despite their numerical disadvantage Britain looked like doing the impossible when Alex Murphy got the try which put Britain ahead with the score at 17–11 with ten minutes to go. Then penalties were given against Britain and a few minutes from time there were four points difference in the score. In Australia they have a timekeeper who blows a hooter or rings a bell when time is up and while we were waiting for it Ken Irvine scored a try in the corner, which British players claimed was from a forward pass. Referee Darcy Lawlor allowed it and with a brilliant kick right from the touchline Irvine converted to give Australia a sensational victory by 18 points to 17.

For the first time on any tour a Sydney club side was played when the St. George team met Britain. There was no letting up by the Lions who were keen to win and did so handsomely, 33–5. Out of 21 games played Britain won 18 and lost three.

They weren't so successful when the Kangaroos came here almost a year later in 1963. On Wednesday, October 16th to be exact, a Test match was played at Wembley Stadium for the first time. Some called it a flop, I didn't, at least not from an experimental viewpoint, though from a playing point of view it probably was. Torrential rain affected the gate, a poor British team was selected and the Australians ran away with victory by 28 points to 2. Star of the match was Reg Gasnier, possibly the best-ever Australian centre and certainly among the all-time greats in any country. "The Gas", as he was called by his team-mates, got a hat-trick of tries. Centre-threequarter Graeme Langlands, a controversial figure right through the tour, kicked five goals.

The worst was still to come, for in November 1963, at Swinton, there was real humiliation for British R.L. A record 50 points was scored by Australia against our 12 and the Ashes were gone. Langlands had seven goals and two tries and Irvine had three of the 12 tries which Australia scored. The third Test had some remarkable scenes and three players were sent off, Brian Hambly and Barry Muir (Australia) and Cliff Watson (Britain). Great Britain won this game by 16 points to 5. The Kangaroos played 22 matches, won 16, lost 5 and drew one. Langlands was the leading scorer with 11 tries and 51 goals from 15 games – 135 points, while Gasnier had 11 tries from 10 matches. It was the first Australian series win in Britain.

It was three years later before the British got their chance of revenge. They made an encouraging start to the 1966 tour when they beat the Kangaroos 17 points to 13 in the first Test at Sydney in June. The Australians had been lifted when Swinton fullback Ken Gowers pulled hours before the match with a rib injury, but his deputy, Hull's Arthur Keegan, was a more than adequate replacement landing three vital goals.

The fierce rivalry between Great Britain and Australia was never far below the surface and controversy marked the second Test at Lang Park, Brisbane in July. Hunslet forward Bill Ramsey got his marching orders for the second time on the tour and stand-in British skipper, forward Brian Edgar, was attacked by a spectator on the pitch.

The British football style was stifled by the attack of temper and they were beaten six points to four. Welsh-born Australian full-back Keith Barnes scored all of their points with three penalties.

Yet another battle between the two protagonists was waged for the third Test back in Sydney later that month. St Helens forward Cliff Watson, voted the fairest and best player in the previous Tests, was sent off for allegedly kicking after six minutes of the second half and British hopes were further dimmed when forward. John Mantle was injured and another forward Dave Robinson laid out in the final minutes.

So Australia won the battle and the war with a 19 points to 14 victory. But nothing could stop the British claiming that Ken Irvine's try that made the score 16 points to 9 for Australia had been preceded with a blatant knock-on. With such stuff are all Great Britain v Australia Test matches punctuated.

Tempers had not noticeably cooled when the Australians arrived in Britain for the next series in 1967. Their Headingley hoodoo of never having won a Test on the ground struck again and they went down 16 points to 11 in the first Test. That defeat was even harder to swallow because they had forward Dennis Manteit sent off for felling British general Roger Millward.

Yet another attempt to introduce big-time Rugby League to London came on 3rd November when the second Test was played at the vast West London stadium, White City. The move away from their native heath did not suit the British who were beaten 17 points to 11 in front of 17,445 spectators. The critical point in the match came when Wakefield's Ian Brooke failed to hold a pass on his own 25 yard line and Australian forward Ron Coote galloped through for a gift try.

The following month the Australians had the satisfaction of winning yet another series on British soil. On a snow and ice affected pitch for the Third Test at Station Road, Swinton, the Kangaroos adapted themselves to the conditions and ran out comfortable winners 11 points to 3 despite having their hooker Noel Kelly sent off for flooring scrum half Tommy Bishop in the second half.

After several years without sight of the ashes Britain's 1970 tour to Australia and New Zealand became more than a matter for national pride. It was a crusade. Immediate hopes that the trend of the 1960s would be reversed crashed when the Australians ran riot in the first Test at Brisbane in June. Their 37 points to 15 victory was very comfortable and a bonus for the Aussies came when Graeme Langlands kicked nine goals to break the peerless Jim Sullivan's record of 62 points in Test matches between the two countries.

But if the Kangaroos had thought that their hold on the Ashes was virtually guaranteed they must have been shaken by subsequent events. The second test at the Sydney Cricket Ground produced a 28 points to 7 landslide for the British with the smallest man on the field, half-back Roger Millward, bagging 20 points for himself – two tries, six goals and a drop goal. Referee Don Lancashire, however, was not very satisfied with every aspect of the British performance for he sent off Leeds centre Syd Hynes after a clash with legendary Aussie forward Artie Beetson. The Yorkshireman could be counted unlucky to be sent off as he was laid out and lost two teeth in the incident.

The deciding Test was played in Sydney during July. The British made the running and, despite a late Australian revival, they emerged winners 21 points to 17. The Kangaroo cause, however, had not been helped when Beetson had been sent off for throwing a punch at Watson.

Despite that incident the standard of play was very high. As I noted in my report to the Sunday Mirror that day, England and Manchester United soccer star Bobby Charlton had been at the game had said: "What a match, what a great win." Bobby is keen on Rugby League and knows what he is talking about.

Again that man Millward had a hand in the victory scoring the last try from a great pass by Doug Laughton. It was a crucial score as the Aussies had crept to within one point of the British score. But the British held on and returned to Europe in triumph with the Ashes.

Australian pressure saw the first Test match of the 1973 series in Britain taken to Wembley. The experiment was a double disappointment for them. There was a meagre crowd of 10,000 which was virtually lost in the Empire Stadium vastness and they were beaten 21 points to 12. Star of the show for the British was Wakefield stand-off Dave Topliss who had played a part in all four tries.

The Australian's dismal record at Headingley was finally laid to rest when they won the second Test of the series there 14 points to six later in November. Graham Eadie, a player who was to figure largely in later Test series with the British, made his Test debut for the Aussies at full-back and was the match of the match kicking five goals. He had taken over from Langlands who broke his hand just before the match. The match was plagued with 70 miles per hour gusts of wind and the Australians used it to their advantage during the second half. Britain were handicapped when Brian Lockwood, the Castleford forward, was sent off for a tackle on Australian halfback Bobby Fulton, another rising Kangaroo star.

Steve Rogers, world
class centre from the
1978 Australian tourists.

Bobby Fulton of Australia tries to find a way round the tackle of Steve Nash (Great Britain). Australian teammate Ray Price looks on anxiously.

The venue for the third and deciding Test Wilderspool Stadium, Warrington was the subject of a gripping frost before the match, but the Australians insisted on playing despite the skating rink conditions.

Britain's players considered the pitch conditions dangerous and their reluctance to play was reflected in the quality of their performance. Beetson, after the game labelled the greatest playing forward by British coach Jim Challinor, and Warrington born Fulton were Australia's men of the moment.

"Bozo" Fulton had stolen a march by acquiring a special kind of rubber soled shoes and he helped inspire the Australian 15 points to five win.

Twelve months later Britain were down-under again. One of the major worries British teams endure when they leave home shores are referees and their different national views of the laws. And all the 1974 tourists fears were realised in the first test at Brisbane in June.

Match official Don Lancashire was severely criticised by coach Challinor after the game for allowing the only Australian try of the match while two British players were lying injured and unattended. It was not satisfaction either when a senior Australian official admitted following Britain's 12 points to six defeat that the referee had been mistaken in not stopping the match for treatment to be given to the injured players.

The famous Sydney Cricket Ground hosted the second Test and this time the Poms had their revenge winning the match 14 points to 11. The British selectors had had a rough time picking a team as they had only 17 fit players available.

John Gray, a forward signed from Coventry Rugby Union club by Wigan, was drafted into the side as hooker because the two position specialists Keith Bridges and Kevin Ashcroft were both injured. He did a superb, courageous job.

After suffering a head injury he had to leave the field for treatment. He returned heavily bandaged but was eventually forced to quit with a finger injury just before the end of the match. The 48,000 crowd gave him a standing ovation recognising the quality of his performance and valour.

Yet another decisive Test was in prospect and the impressive Sydney venue the battlefield. Gray, using his round-the-corner goalkicking style kicked six goals for Britian but it was not enough to stop the Australians winning the match 22 points to 18. The breaking point came when big Aussie forward Bob McCarthy intercepted a pass from British stand off Ken Gill to score a killer try.

The balance of Test power was firmly planted in the southern hemisphere after this trio of matches, and the next series in October and November of 1978 did little to dispel that view.

In the first Test at Wigan both scrum halves, Steve Nash for Britain and old rival Tom Raudonikis for Australia, were sent off for fighting and it was the British who suffered most.

Without the battling Salford halfback the Lions were beaten 15 points to 9 and not even a spectacular try by Warrington's Welsh winger John Bevan could lift the gloom.

That first Test defeat and an injury to hooker David Ward of Leeds forced the British selectors to think again about their team. Their decision to introduce veterans Jim Mills (Widnes), Tony Fisher (Bradford), and Brian Lockwood (Hull) into the forwards was greeted with derision in Australia.

Taunts of British being a "Dad's Army" after the BBC-TV comedy series about an elderly Home Guard platoon came winging across the oceans. Amazingly, lifted by the faith of controversial Bradford coach Peter Fox, the "experienced" British team won the second Test 18 points to 14 at Odsal Stadium, Bradford.

The series was set for a grand stand finish, but somebody forgot to tell the British. More than 30,000 fans packed into Headingley to see the Australians run riot in a 23 points to 6 victory and the ease of their win shook the British game to its very foundations.

With the parent country's game still shouting loudly about the need to re-think their approach to the sport a number of younger, less experienced players were included in the British party for the 1979 tour to Australian and New Zealand. The storm clouds, however, were gathering thick and fast as they arrived to face the Kangaroos.

The obvious fitness gap between the virtually full-time professional Australian players and the British part-timers was still growing and it developed into a major embarrassment for the once-proud, Poms.

All the signs were there when they were massacred 35 points to nil in the first Test at Brisbane. Australian centre Mick Cronin had his eyes firmly on the target as he kicked ten incredible goals to add to their five tries. Wakefield forward Trevor Skerrett was sent off ten minutes from time for an alleged stiff-arm tackle.

Later in June the second Test was played at Sydney and, although British pride was restored with a better points return, they still slipped to a 24 points to 16 defeat. That left a dis-spirited British team heading for the Third Test in Sydney in July facing the virtually unknown prospect of a whitewash.

And with the "Poms" on the rack the Kangaroos put the boot in. In front of 16,844 spectators, the lowest gate for a Test between the two countries in Australia, the Australians had another field day winning 28 points to two.

Nothing the British players could do was right while the deadly boot of Cronin (eight goals) and four tries boosted the Aussies. The British party could boast that it did not lose any of the provincial matches but in a sport where Test matches count for everything that claim counted for little or nothing.

Perhaps the only British consolation was that they had discovered two promising international stand off halves Steve Evans (Featherstone Rovers) and John Woods (Leigh). Now the British authorities will have to review their attitudes towards the game and international Rugby if they are to remove the Aussie boot from their neck. The traditional dependence on football skills to beat Australian brawn has failed, now the British boys will have to be fit as well.

# 7
# THE NEW ZEALAND TESTS

New Zealand have always lived under the shadow of Australia so far as English tours are concerned. When a Great Britain tour to New Zealand follows an arduous Australian trip there is always a feeling of "the end in sight", and some of the games are used to give the "ham and eggers" the chance to get a Test place. "Ham-and-eggers" is the name given to the boys who usually play in the country games on tour but rarely in the big matches.

Another factor is that the Test pitch at Carlow Park, Auckland, is a former Chinese gardener's plot and not the best-drained ground in the world. This brings a lesser quality to the football and with a staleness at times in some players the tour has not had the happy results which might have been expected. It is thought in some quarters that a tour "Down under" might with advantage start in New Zealand rather than in Australia and there might be something in this.

In the two Tests of 1962 New Zealand won both. In the 1958 Tests each side had a win. In 1954 Great Britain won the series by two to one, the (14–20) defeat coming at Greymouth, the first and only time a Test was played there. It was given the game as a tribute to the fine work put in by West Coast officials like Tom McKenzie, but it wasn't good enough for a Test match.

The 1950 Tests were shared and in 1946, when only one Test was played in Auckland, New Zealand won by 13 points to 8. This, I think, indicates my view about the British approach to New Zealand Tests. In most of these defeats, although there were the usual rows about officials' decisions, New Zealand deserved to win.

New Zealand tours to this country have been spasmodic and until recently provided problems. After the first, in 1907–8, there wasn't another until 1926. And it was a disastrous one. The team, based at Harrogate, had trouble in camp and a group of "rebels" went on strike; when the party returned to New Zealand some of them were suspended for life. And it meant life, for in 1950 I remember one of the suspended players coming to see if I could help to get them reinstated – "Just to clear our names before we die," said one. Thirty-four matches were played on this tour, 16 being won by the visitors and 18 lost. The failure of the trip had such an adverse effect on the code in New Zealand that they did not feel equipped to send a team again until thirteen years later.

Unfortunately, the tours to this country have had more than their share of bad luck, none more so that the 1939

1st Test, Great Britain v New Zealand at Swinton, 8.11.55.

New Zealand forward Maxwell goes over the line for the first try of the match despite the attentions of Great Britain forwards Wilkinson and Foster.

tour, which had a good party with Jack Redwood as manager. One match had been played at St. Helens and won by the New Zealanders when war was declared. The party were in Blackpool helping to fill sandbags when the ban on sport was lifted. I was then manager of Dewsbury and at 9 a.m., on Friday, September 8th, 1939, received permission to play a match against the New Zealand team at Crown Flatt. The Kiwis were willing to play and with an all night chase for a team and match arrangements to make I managed to get the game on. It made international news for it was the only organised sport of any kind played in England that day, the spectators carrying their gas mask cases to the match. New Zealand won 22–10.

It was a heartbreaking job for New Zealand to carry the financial burden of the tour costs and it took another

New Zealand determination captured in a picture from the first RL Test at Headingley. A breakaway by Lee, the Kiwis second row forward.

New Zealand v Great Britain. Edwards crosses the line to score with R. S. Cooke and M. I. Cooke following.

eight years before they were ready to travel here again. This time their luck changed and with a terrific side, well managed and with A. T. McClymont as coach, they played 27 matches, won 16, lost 10 and drew one. They were unlucky not to take the Test series, for it was a one-point win for Britain at Headingley in the first Test by 11 to 10. They won the Swinton Test but lost the rubber when Britain won easily at Odsal Stadium 25–9. With a good goal-kicking full-back in Warwick Clarke, a strong, British type centre in Morrie Robertson, great forwards in Charlie McBride, Jack Newton, Travers Hardwick and Pat Smith, it was a side which put New Zealand back into world reckoning. This was proved when recently the world ratings of all Test matches between France, Britain, Australia and New Zealand were reckoned – it was the Kiwis who headed the unofficial world list.

The next team came in 1951–2 and returned with a good record to show for the visit. Twenty-eight played, 18 won and 10 lost. But they hadn't a Test win, although they were again very unlucky with a one-point defeat,

20–19, at Swinton in the second Test. The 1955 tour was not as good, although New Zealand slammed in a victory of 28 points to 12 in the third Test with the Ashes lost. They did the same also at Leeds in the first Test in 1961, winning 29–11, their biggest-ever score against a national British team. It was of no avail, for Britain took the next two Tests. This side played the lowest number of games on the six full tours, having 11 wins out of only 20 matches.

The eighth New Zealand tour was staged in England in 1965 when the Kiwis, captained by experienced scrum-half Bill Snowdon, played 23 matches with 13 wins, nine defeats and one draw. The drawn game 9-9 was the third Test at Wigan and the best of the three matches played, the first two being won by Britain. Best player on tour, voted for by different judges at each game, was 1961 Kiwi skipper, Don Hammond.

It was another six years before the Kiwis returned to tour Britain in the autumn of 1971. Their captain was Roy Christian, one of New Zealand's most respected players and captains as well as a distant relation to Fletcher Christian of Mutiny on the Bounty fame.

New Zealand's position as one of Rugby League's international second class citizens lulled the British into a false sense of security and they were to discover that this was an outstanding Kiwi team with world class players like prop Henry Tatana, scrum half Ken Stirling and winger Phil Orchard.

For the first Test at Salford on 25th September Great Britain were tipped as clear favourites by the home press, but the Kiwis surprised everybody by winning 18 points to 13.

The second Test at Castleford on 16th October had more than its fair share of controversy. The British stormed into a 11–0 lead but then their troubles started.

First the New Zealanders reduced their arrears to one point and then the British lost out on two chances to pull away when referee Deryk Brown ruled that touch-downs by centres John Walsh and Bill Benyon did not count because they had failed to ground the ball properly.

Then, to add insult to Britain's injury, Mr Brown

allowed a try by Kiwi winger Orchard to stand, despite British players' claims that he had stepped into touch before scoring.

The New Zealanders won the Test 17 points to 14 and it gave them the series, the first that an all New Zealand party had ever won in Britain. Again the attendance for the match was disappointing. Just over 3,700 had seen the first Test and the second had attracted 4,108.

In the third Test at Headingley on 6th November Great Britain took consolation with a 12 points to 3 win, but it did little to sweeten the bitter taste of a series defeat by the previously unrated amateurs from New Zealand.

New Zealand tours of this country have never been frequent. Their all-amateur status means that their ability to afford more regular tours has been less than their more prosperous professional neighbours from across the Tasman Sea, Australia.

*Opposite:* Kiwis v Great Britain. Captain Roy Christian near to tears is chaired off the field by jubilant teammates.

Lord Derby, President of the English Rugby League meets New Zealand captain Roy Christian prior to the match. Introducing is the manager of the Kiwis Mr. Jack Williams.

That explains why the Kiwis' next European tour was not staged until the autumn of 1980. Before the trip they played Test series against the Australians and, although they did not win, it clearly influenced the playing style of the tourists.

From the opening game at Blackpool, British commentators were struck by the free-running, similarities between the Kiwis and the 1978 Australian tourists. It should have been obvious from that point that they were going to be formidable opponents.

For the first Test on 18th October at Wigan, the British selectors were still trying to find the right blend following the two disastrous series against the Australians. In came wingers Chris Camilleri (Barrow), Keith Bentley (Widnes), stand off Steve Hartley (Hull KR) and second row forward Les Gorley (Widnes) while the captaincy was handed to full-back George Fairbairn, Wigan's Scottish player-coach.

Fairbairn, playing in front of his own supporters, suffered the indignity of having the ball knocked out of his hands while diving over the line for what looked to be a certain try.

Winger Dane O'Hara had hit him with a last-ditch tackle just as Fairbairn was airborne and that almost certainly saved the game for New Zealand. Guided by the silky-skilled stand off half Fred Ah Kuoi the Kiwis led 10 points to 9 at halftime and only a desperate performance by the makeshift British team drew the match 14 points each. The New Zealanders, however, had made their mark.

If anybody had missed that point at Wigan they could not have failed to be impressed in the second Test at Odsal, Bradford on 2nd November.

After one of the poorest ever British international performances in League history the Kiwis walked away with the spoils 12 points to 8 and had it not been for the brave defence of Fairbairn the margin of victory would certainly have been greater.

Between the second and third Tests the New Zealanders travelled down to London to play the Great Britain Under 24 side at Craven Cottage, home of Rugby League's capital city club Fulham who joined the League for the 1980–81 campaign. A paltry crowd of 2,500 suffered the bitterly cold weather to see the tourists win 18 points to 14, but the success of players like Widnes full-back Mick Burke and Oldham loose forward Terry Flanagan earned them a place in the squad for the third and final Test at Headingley.

Burke actually played in the match because Fairbairn was injured and he played a major role in the British performance. The captaincy was handed over to Hull KR forward Len Casey and Whitehaven scrum half Arnie Walker took over from Kevin Dick for his first international honour at the age of 27.

Determined to take their second successive series in Britain the Kiwis were tough opponents, but two spectacular tries by Leigh's Jamaican-born winger Des Drummond gave Britain the match 10 points to two. That gave Britain a share of the series and saved their blushes.

Although the Kiwis had been forced to share the series their stylish players had made a great impact on the British clubs and there was a scramble to sign some of their players. The powerful Hull club moved quickly in a bid to recruit Ah Kuoi, the outstanding player of the series, centre James Leulai and winger O'Hara. Ah Kuoi chose to join Australian club North Sydney, but, at the time of writing the Airlie Birds are still confident of signing O'Hara and Leulai.

# 8
# KANGAROOS, KIWIS AND SPRINGBOKS IN ENGLAND

When New Zealand players like George Smith, Lance Todd and Australian Albert Rosenfeld toured England in 1908 with the first touring team they liked England and what it had to offer so much that they returned to play for English League clubs. Smith went to Oldham, Rosenfeld to Huddersfield and Todd joined Wigan. They were among the first of many overseas players who domiciled themselves in the British Isles.

One of the clubs to show a special interest in Antipodean players, and particularly Australians, is Leeds. No doubt their chairman, Sir Edwin Airey, who had a showman's flair for the development of Headingley, had much to do with it, but as early as 1912 an Australian by the name of "Dinny" Campbell was offered to Leeds and can be said to have set the pattern.

"Dinny", who cost Leeds a £350 signing fee and, initially, £2 a match, scored his first try for Leeds against Bramley in September 1912. He had 16 tries to his credit that season. His last try for Leeds was eight years later, when he ran through nearly the whole of the Wigan team from his own twenty-five line. In 258 games he scored 136 tries and kicked three goals. A great signing for Leeds and the forerunner of many star Australians.

An Australian was the most prolific try-scorer Leeds ever had – Eric Harris, who averaged one a match, actually 391 tries in 383 matches, a remarkable record. Known as the "Toowoomba Ghost", he came from that beautiful Darling Downs town of Toowoomba which I know so well. He was a tall, lean man who appeared to glide through the opposition on the right wing.

A year or two ago in Brisbane, Eric and I chatted about English and Australian Rugby League. His end in English football was rather sudden and many thought he would have years of playing in Australia, but he did not stay in the game long afterwards. He told me why. He was still a fast runner but had lost control of his pace. In his hey-day his acceleration was his greatest attribute and he could gauge to the inch when and where he could beat an opponent.

Harris joined Leeds in 1930 and quickly got into his stride in every way, running in 58 tries in his first season. On the opposite flank was a Yorkshire winger, Stan Smith, who scored 29 tries that winter. The Harris-Smith combination of leading try scorers continued at the top of the Leeds list until 1938–9.

Harris had nine glorious seasons at Headingley. After his first 58 tries he followed on with 41, 55, 24, 45, 63 and 40. He also kicked 16 goals for Leeds to bring his points tally to a magnificent 1,205. Generously, he told me he owed much to his two principal centres during his spell with Leeds; his countryman Jeff Moores, who later joined York, and a namesake, Lancastrian centre from Leigh, Fred Harris.

The winger nearest to Eric Harris's record of a try a match was a Scot from Hawick, Drew Turnbull. A leg injury put Turnbull out of football early, yet in 208 games for the Leeds club he scored 206 tries. With Stanley Smith scoring 186 out of 261 games there were a lot of points from these three wingers, Harris, Turnbull and Smith.

Most of the Australians who joined Leeds were successes. One of the unfortunate ones was Joe "Chimpy" Busch, a scrum half who had figured prominently for Australia in Test football here in 1929. When Busch joined Leeds, at the same time as Eric Harris, the club's regular scrum half, Les Adams, hit top form and it became almost an embarrassment to have the two internationals. Busch scored 26 tries in 137 games and when Adams left Leeds he came into his own. Among other things he starred in a dramatic Yorkshire Cup Final against Wakefield; there were two draws before Joe Busch got his Cup winners' medal.

Prior to the arrival of Eric Harris at Headingley, another Australian, a well-built, classy centre named Frank O'Rourke, had headed the try lists. He had 20 in the 1927–8 season, followed by a 26 and a 27, with, incidentally, fellow-Australian Jeff Moores second with 20.

After the war, Leeds took on big Arthur Clues, who had been sent off in the 1946 third Test at Sydney for having a swing at Joe Egan, the Great Britain hooker. When Clues asked referee Tom McMahon why he had been sent off, for he missed hitting Egan, McMahon reportedly told him, "That's why – you missed him!"

Clues became a buddy of New Zealand's dynamic full-back, Bert Cook and the pair stayed on in England. Clues, a second row forward, scored 75 tries for Leeds and played in 236 matches. He moved on to Hunslet while Cook went to Keighley.

Until the ban was imposed, which it is periodically, Leeds kept an interest in the Australian market and signed a young half-back with whom I had been impressed in Brisbane in 1946 called Teddy Verrenkamp. Teddy scored 68 tries before he moved to Keighley, and later returned to coach the Queensland State team.

Before the ban was finally imposed Leeds had signed Keith McLellan, a centre from Sydney Rugby Union, and Bob McMaster, a wrestler and prop forward from Queensland. Although McMaster was signed on a short-term contract he managed 179 games, 13 tries and 13 goals.

Centre Keith McLellan, a good captain and sportsman, played exactly 100 games and scored 32 tries for Leeds. He captained the Leeds team to a Cup win at Wembley in 1957 and not many Australians have done that. The McLellan family settled well in Leeds, where Keith became a schoolteacher, before returning to Wollongong in New South Wales.

Australians and New Zealand players have done well with Leeds, which is the only venue in England where international Rugby League is played along with cricket between Australia and England. The main stand is a double-jointed effort, one side to watch cricket and the other to see League games.

"We need a crack Australian footballer to put Leigh on the map." The speaker was James Hilton, chairman of Leigh football club, and the conversation took place with me in the Australia Hotel, Sydney. Mr. Hilton, a power behind the revival of the Leigh club, was in Australia as a visitor with the 1950 touring team. He told me that everyone in Australia knew of Leeds but had rarely heard of Leigh. "When I'm asked where I come from and answer Leigh, they always say 'Oh yes, Leeds in Yorkshire.' I've got to put Leigh on the football map and the only way to do it is to sign a top Australian Rugby Union player," said Mr. Hilton.

After long discussions he decided on my advice to go for Trevor Allan, captain of the Australian Rugby Union team and a player who could tackle and would run straight, important features in the professional game. Negotiations were opened and thanks to Ray Stehr, the former crack Australian forward, progress was made. The offer to Trevor was £5,000 and as the contract period wasn't a long one it tempted him to sign.

In 1947, a five-year ban agreement was made between the English league and the Australian Board of Control which stopped any player going from one country to another. Just before the ban took effect, two Australians signed for English clubs – Test winger Lionel Cooper and full-back John Hunter.

The Huddersfield club had asked me on my return from Australia if I would get them Cooper, who had scored a great try in the first Test on the Sydney cricket ground in 1946. I had spoken to Lionel and he voiced one stipulation: he wanted a travelling companion. I had been impressed in Sydney with the young, dashing type of full-back Johnny Hunter and suggested he should come with Cooper. Eventually the deal was done, the pair costing Huddersfield only £1,500, a remarkable signing for the Fartown club, probably the best they ever made. Cooper scored 432 tries at Huddersfield, which was a record for the club, and in one game, against Keighley, created another record of ten tries and two goals. Hunter was brilliant and one of the most popular players ever to wear the famous claret and gold jersey. Both he and Cooper returned to Australia after many years' valuable service.

In addition to Cooper and Hunter I also arranged for the signing of Don Graham, a half-back, to come to Hunslet and "Dinny" Boocker, a winger, to Wakefield Trinity. Ray Stehr, my contact man, also arranged for half-back Pat Devery to sign for Huddersfield. Harry Bath, a big forward, joined Barrow, Bob Bartlett, a centre, signed for Bramley while Leeds bought winger Len Kenny.

Although more Australians have signed for English clubs than from any other country there has been some good signings from New Zealand. The first batch came with the pioneering boys who had been over with the "All Blacks" Rugby Union team and later toured with Baskerville's party.

The 1947 ban also included New Zealand players, but a few had signed before it became effective. The best of this era was Cecil Mountford, who came from the mining town of Blackball near Greymouth on the west coast of the South Island. An excellent stand-off, his play was typically English and he had successful spells at Wigan and Warrington, where he became manager. He later returned to New Zealand to coach Rugby League.

Because of the ban on R.L. signings some English clubs searched and found good Rugby Union players. One of these was Bert Cook. "Cooky" had been in England with a successful Services team and was returning home when I met him travelling from North Island to South Island. We chatted about rugby and I thought at the time he was more than knowledgeable on Rugby League football affairs. I learnt the reason soon after when he signed for Leeds and kicked many brilliant goals for the club. All in all he kicked 556 and scored 19 tries, to amass the total of 1,169 points from 210 games.

Bradford also entered the New Zealand market, sending over their chairman Harry Hornby to find some players. He brought four back to England: Joe Phillips, full-back, Norman Hastings, winger, Bill Dickson, half-back, and Bill Hawes, centre. Of this quartet Phillips was the only one who stayed in England for a long spell, moving after a most successful period with Bradford to Keighley, where he became captain.

Bradford's next signing from New Zealand was also a good one. They persuaded Jack McLean, the "All-Black" winger, to turn professional and he scored many tries in English R.L., leading the League list in 1956 with 64.

Peter Henderson, another "All-Black" winger, played in seven Rugby Union Tests before turning professional. He signed for Huddersfield in 1950 and scored 214 tries in 258 matches. Recently he applied to be reinstated by the New Zealand R.U. authority, but despite having achieved some good coaching results in the Union game since his return he was refused. His case recalls George Nepia, possibly the greatest name in New Zealand Rugby Union. He was the Maori full-back star who played at Twickenham against England in 1924. Thirteen years later he caused a sensation by signing professional forms for the newly formed London R.L. club, Streatham and Mitcham, but later returned home to become a R.U. referee. Before he did so he had a spell with Halifax, who have signed quite a few New Zealand players from time to time. Two good centres have been Charlie Smith and Tommy Lynch.

In the 1940s, Wigan took on a New Zealand winger in Brian Nordgren, who qualified as a barrister at Liverpool University before returning to New Zealand. I met Nordgren in Queen St., Auckland, in 1962 and he was still talking about the goal he missed for Wigan in the 1946 Cup Final in the dying seconds, which would have won the match had he kicked it. Wigan had earlier signed a number of the 1926 tour players in Maori forward Len Mason, centre Ben Davidson and winger Lou Brown. These were followed by another trio when St. Helens stepped into the New Zealand market and bought winger Roy Hardgrave and forwards Len Hutt and Trevor Hall to Knowsley Road, the home of the St. Helens club. Unlike Brown and Mason, who won Cup winners' medals in 1929, the St. Helens trio had to be content with losers' awards a year later when the Saints were beaten by Widnes.

English Rugby League would not have been as good without the New Zealanders and it is well to remember that it was a N.Z. man who brought the first touring team to England.

One country where there is no ban on players signing for English clubs is South Africa. But although a few gold nuggets in the shape of footballers have been found there they haven't been so numerous as was once hoped. I reckon that in the last decade alone over fifty players have been signed by English league clubs but only about half a dozen have been "winners". The cost to the clubs and the game has been around £200,000. In pre-war football Wigan found two good players in van Heerden, a winger, and van Rooyen, a forward, while in recent years the best of the South African signings has been Tom van Vollenhoven (see page 119). Other successes were Fred Griffiths, a good full-back signing for Wigan where he kicked many goals, while Alan Skene and Colin Greenwood did good service with Wakefield before going to play in Sydney. Wakefield also bought Jan Prinsloo from St. Helens, though he didn't stay long, and St. Helens found another good winger in Len Killeen. Winger Will Rosenberg had a lot of success with Leeds then transferred to Hull.

Unfortunately there have been far more S.A. failures than successes. Barrow, Hull, Workington and Whitehaven had several signings but the players weren't happy in League football. Leigh also tried a few but they didn't click and the same thing was experienced by York.

"I was too old and too cold", said Iron Man Ivor Dorrington when he explained his inability to make the grade at forward with Wakefield, and one can sympathise with him.

A Rhodesian player who came and conquered is Trevor Lake, the dashing Wigan winger who scored two magnificent tries at Wembley in 1965 and was the leading try scorer of that season. Lake came with full-back John Winton, who found more success when he moved to Oldham.

An effort to start Rugby League in South Africa was made some years ago and the 1962 Great Britain touring team called there to play exhibition games on their way home. Unfortunately there were two governing bodies instead of just one and with the normal opposition from Rugby Union on matters of grounds it never really got started. Another effort is being made.

Rugby Union playing countries are always a target for R.L. scouts. Even Fiji. When I saw a Fijian R.U. team playing in 1950 in Sydney I was impressed by a wing-threequarter named Jo Levula. Years later he was signed as a professional player by Rochdale Hornets. They quickly followed up by taking on the Fijian R.U. captain, centre Orisi Dwai, and several others, making quite a Fijian colony in the cotton town. The British climate is probably against a continued success of Fijian imports but they certainly add colour to the game.

Regarding France, there is an understanding that French players will not be brought over to play with English clubs, but we can import from Italy. Forward Tony Rossi joined Wigan and Blackpool and seems to like Lancashire.

What would be really interesting would be to see how players of the American code fared over here, without their protective clothing of course. So far there has been one signing, but he didn't stay long.

# 9
# FOUR ALL-TIME GREATS

## 1: Harold Wagstaff

Not many sportsmen become immortal; men of the Stan Matthews, Joe Louis and Don Bradman calibre are few. One of Rugby League's all time "greats" was Harold Wagstaff, affectionately known as "Ahr Waggy". Five golden guineas were paid by Huddersfield in 1906 to sign the local youth who became a world-renowned centre-threequarter. Born in May, 1891, he was playing for Huddersfield's first team by the time he was fifteen and was only seventeen when he turned out for England in a Test against Australia. A master strategist, Wagstaff introduced what some people called scientific obstruction. He described it as the standing pass, a move which had a remarkable and advantageous effect on the game. It was simple enough: he merely turned his back on an approaching opponent as he passed the ball.

"Waggy" had great success in Australia, though his team did not win the Ashes when they toured in 1920. His big Test success was in 1914 when England took the Ashes after the third and deciding match which came to be known as "Rorke's Drift", after the famous last stand against the Zulus. Wagstaff led a crippled team to a 14–6 victory in a game still written and talked about by those who remember it.

"England expects every man to do his duty" read a cable from home just before the match and Wagstaff said that many of the players had tears in their eyes and battle in their hearts as they walked out on to the Sydney cricket ground. Within minutes of the start England's winger Frank Williams twisted his knee, but by half time they were leading 9–3. Soon after the restart Douglas Clarke, a Huddersfield colleague of Wagstaff and a Cumberland wrestler, broke his collar-bone. He returned after treatment but later both he and Williams had to leave the field. The next English casualty was Oldham centre Bill Hall, with concussion. Ten players against thirteen looked to be a hopeless task, then with eighteen minutes to go the miracle happened. Wagstaff found an opening and passed the ball to "Chick" Johnson of Widnes, who although a forward was playing on the wing. Johnson realised he hadn't the speed to run clear so he dropped the ball and starting dribbling. He had forty yards to go but kept dribbling like a soccer star, beating man after man and scoring a great try which was converted by full-back Albert Wood. Although Australia scored near the end victory was assured and the 14–6 victory was one of the greatest ever. Wagstaff and his team-mates were cheered by the Sydney crowd as they left the ground.

Harold Wagstaff's official Test career ran from his first at Newcastle in 1911 to his last on a muddy ground at Salford in 1922. He played in only nine Test matches but undoubtedly the outbreak of war prevented him from making more appearances in the English jersey.

A fine tactician – I·sat next to him at the 1939 Cup Final and his quiet comments were an education – Harold did a great deal for the development of Rugby League and his classic style of play justly earned him the title "Prince of Centres".

## 2: Jim Sullivan

Jim Sullivan was Rugby League's finest-ever full-back. In almost 25 seasons and three Australian tours he scored over 6,000 points – 2,959 goals and 96 tries.

When Wigan signed the tall young man from Cardiff Rugby Union in 1921 they did not realise they had taken on one of the greats-to-be in R.L. He was eighteen then and stayed in the game a long, long time. In fact he was still playing in wartime football and turned out under my managership in many matches. I remember Jim didn't like to lose, however unimportant the game; nor did he like being rested even on tour; he just wanted to play in all the games he could. Although remaining officially on the Wigan books he "guested" with Dewsbury in many matches and played for them in the Yorkshire Cup Final of 1941 at Huddersfield against Bradford.

Sullivan's Test run against Australia began in 1924 at Sydney. It continued until 1933 with only one break, the first Test of the 1929 Australian tour in England, when he was dropped for the only time in his career. Britain were soundly beaten 31–8 and needless to say Sullivan was recalled for the remaining games.

Jim's Australian successes are numerous and so are his records. The story is told of a Test match on the Sydney cricket ground when he was playing for England. In the first minute a big cheer went up and the crowd outside the ground, locked out, asked what had happened. "Sullivan kicked a goal from the half-way line," they were told. Back came the reply, "Oh! I thought he must have missed one." Sully didn't like missing any.

Sullivan was a big fellow, over 6 ft. and at his heaviest 16 stone, and many of his tries were scored down the blind side of the scrum. Some fans say he wouldn't have had the same success these days when full backs don't kick, but I wouldn't accept that. He was a master footballer who could have adapted himself to whatever rules he played under.

Jim was Britain's leading individual goal-kicker for many years until Bernard Ganley of Oldham set a season record with 224 goals in 1957. But I doubt if any player will ever pass the 6,206 points mark, which goes behind the name of Jim Sullivan, Wigan, Wales and England.

After his playing career ended Jim became coach to Wigan, then caused a sensation by moving to St. Helens where he had much to do with the development of the sixteen-year-old starlet scrum-half, Alex Murphy.

## 3: Billy Boston

Billy Boston cried the day he quit Rugby League.

Everyone in the game should have followed suit, for

Billy Boston, Wigan and Great Britain in full flight with Swinton number one Ken Gowers (right) coming across to attempt at tackling.

this was the end of an era, the retirement of one of the greatest personalities Rugby has ever reared.

When Cardiff born Billy burst like a bomb into the game in 1954, 8,000 turned up at Central Park to see him play ... in an 'A' team game. They were not disappointed!

Six first team games later Billy was chosen for the Great Britain tour of Australia and New Zealand.

He broke the tour try-scoring record with 36!

So was launched Boston's international career that did more to put Wigan on the map than their celebrated pier!

By the time 11,000 watched his farewell at Central Park in April 1968 Boston's try-haul was fast-approaching 600–230 more than the previous Wigan record held by Johnny Ring.

And everyone who had seen Billy during his fourteen-year career had marvelled at the class that went with his crunch.

Billy Boston tackling

There was no more fearsome sight than Boston, head down, going for the line.

No more forbidding prospect for a centre than to know Boston was bent on a crash-tackle.

Yet Boston, at 5 ft 10 in. and 15 st. was agile enough to be able to beat his man by sleight of foot.

He had no sleight of hand! The kit-bags he called mitts were power-packed to brush off the opposition.

Eight clubs were in the chase for Boy Boston before Wigan won the race in March 1953 with a £3,000 cheque and patience to match.

Soldier-boy Boston was a prize catch; the star of the Army champions, Catterick's Royal Signals; and scorer of 126 tries in one Army season.

No wonder Wigan crowed when his signing was announced five months after Boston had actually put pen to paper: "The greatest capture we have ever made."

Boston had three brushes with Central Park authority in his life-time.

Once he was suspended, twice he was transfer-listed.

And once his speed went there was talk of pushing him into the pack.

He would have made it too.

But thank goodness power-house Billy ended as he began . . . pounding the wing for Wigan!

## 4: Tom Van Vollenhoven

There'll never be another "Van". And there'll never be truer words than those Tom Van Vollenhoven uttered the day he took his first look at St. Helens and Knowsley Road.

"Show me the line," he told an impromptu Press conference, "and I'll go for it."

Every Rugby League team in the land knows now that that was no idle boast.

Four-hundred tries in the eleven illustrious seasons are mute testimony to Van's class.

Class that put him alongside Brian Bevan, Alf Ellaby, Billy Boston and Lionel Cooper as the greatest wingers of all time.

It cost Saints £4,000 to lure Vollenhoven out of South Africa in September 1957.

The welter of words that preceded the ex-Pretorian policeman to Lancashire promised Rugby League fans a treat.

He'd already made his mark in Rugby Union. He played in all five tests against the Lions of 1955 and gave that famous Irishman Tony O'Reilly a roasting in most of them. Then he toured Australia and New Zealand and won four more caps.

But for the cynics who inhabit Rugby League that wasn't enough. "Let's wait and see" they sneered.

They didn't have long to wait.

Two weeks after his arrival and after only one look at the professional game Saints threw "Van" in at the deep end against Leeds.

More than 20,000 packed Knowsley Road that October day to run the rule over Vollenhoven.

They saw him give away one try and, a minute from time, race 40 yards for a touch-down that in the years to come would be labelled "typical Vollenhoven".

South African Tom Van Vollenhoven who played for St. Helens moves into make a tackle.

Even in this first game it was easy to see that this man had everything a winger needed; perfect running style, balance, speed and fly-paper fingers.

Add courage to that lot – any Rugby League forward who has tried to bundle Vollenhoven into touch will testify to his bravery – and you have the perfect craftsman.

After that first match, Jim Sullivan, who was not given to idle praise, said: "We've seen nothing yet. This lad is going to be a sensation."

How much of a sensation was seen two months later when he equalled Steve Llewellyn's club record of six tries in a game . . . against Wakefield Trinity of all people.

Van finished that first season with 40 tries. The following season he scored 62 tries to shatter Alf Ellaby's club record of 55, a figure that had stood for almost 30 years.

No one now questioned that the "Van" was the most exciting personality to hit Rugby for years. A match-winner, a crowd-puller, and, as Jim Sullivan promised, a sensation.

The "Van" played his last game at Knowsley Road on April 25, 1968.

Almost 16,000 were there to see him win the player-of-the-match award in the 23–10 play-off triumph over Warrington.

A week later Hull K.R. were to spoil the fairy-tale ending to Vollenhoven's career when they beat St. Helens in the championship semi-final.

The "Van" would have dearly loved to go out on the high-note of a championship triumph.

Great moments – he's won every honour the game has to offer – litter "Van's" Rugby life.

But the one he rates the greatest came at Wembley in 1961 when he scored a memorable try to help Saints beat Wigan.

Few who saw it will forget that 70 yard link-up with Ken Large that virtually settled the Cup's destination.

For me, Vollenhoven's greatest try was the one he scored at Odsal Stadium in the Championship final of 1959 against Hunslet. It had every ingredient of greatness.

And if there are still any doubts lingering about Vollenhoven, possibly the truest measure of his worth came from the Saints' fans in the days before he, his wife and three children left for South Africa.

The £2,800 testimonial cheque Van received at the end of June was a Rugby League record. In presenting it Saints' chairman Harry Cook called him the "greatest ever" winger.

Few will argue. There'll never be another Van!

# 10
# THE WELSH

Who is the greatest Welshman ever to come north? That's impossible to say, for it can only be opinion. What is certain is that more backs have succeeded than forwards, no doubt due to the difference in the two codes where Rugby Union forwards play differently from Rugby League pack men. The R.U. style with its line-out requirements is one consideration and the physical need in League has often proved a stumbling block to the development of forwards.

In recent years the two most surprising instances of Welsh Rugby Union converts not adapting well have been former British international captain Russel Robins and Peter Davies. Another "Lions" skipper, Irishman Robin Thompson, also made the change when he joined Warrington, but he, too, could never find his best form. Ill health did not help and eventually he had to give up the game.

Welsh players, backs and forwards alike, often return to their native heath. Not all, mind you. One of the big successes in Rugby League for Leeds in their glorious days was Joe Thompson, who stayed in the North to work for the Leeds Corporation after he had kicked 862 goals and scored 53 tries. He wasn't the only one who stayed and prospered.

Wales provided a great Britain tour captain in Dick Williams, who skippered the 1954 team, and, of course, the immortal Gus Risman in 1946. Risman's career spanned 27 seasons and he scored more than 3,000 points.

Although it has never been possible to establish the Rugby League game as a permanency in South Wales, and many efforts have been made, there is a lot of association between England and Wales where Rugby is concerned. In almost every phase of Rugby League a Welshman strides through the scenes, leaving an undeniable, emphatic imprint on the field.

When Leeds met Bradford Northern at Wembley in 1947 in the Challenge Cup Final, thirteen players came from Wales1 Leeds had Tommy Cornelius, Greth Price and T. L. Williams in the threequarter line, a complete half-back pair in Dick Williams and Dai Jenkins; Dai Prosser and Con Murphy in the front row and Ike Owens at loose forward. Bradford had Emlyn Walters on the wing, the mighty Willie Davies from Penclawd, the cockle village on the Gower coast, at stand-off, and Frank Whitcombe, Trevor Foster and Hagan Evans in the forwards. A mighty Cup contribution and rarely has a Final gone without a Welshman being around. An exception was in 1951, when Wigan met Barrow.

Of the twelve touring teams to go to Australia and New Zealand from these shores three have been captained by Welshmen. In addition to Williams and Risman, there was Jim Sullivan, captain in 1932, who made three trips altogether and would have made a record fourth but turned down the invitation.

Australian followers in the main reckon a Welshman was the greatest ever loose forward sent from England – Ike Owens. This is not an opinion shared by English followers but it is a strong feeling in Sydney, due mainly to some brilliant football in 1946 by Owens in a N.S.W. match and the Test match on the Sydney cricket ground. The hard, fast grounds certainly suited Owens who was a star on that tour. This was a touring side which had a pretty full representation from Wales; led by Risman, the Welshmen in support were winger Arthur Bassett, who had a particularly good second Test at Brisbane; Willie Davies and Dai Jenkins, the half-back pair; full back Joe Jones; centre Ted Ward, from Ammanford, and forwards Frank Whitcombe, Doug Phillips, W. Hughes, I. Owens and Trevor Foster. Eleven out of twenty-six,

Gus Risman, one of Rugby League's greatest imports from Welsh Rugby Union. Player with Salford and then player-coach at Wokington Town. Still lives in Cumbria.

though I believe Doug Phillips was the only man who could speak Welsh!

On earlier tours great players like Johnny Rogers, a scrum half of more than average ability, goal-kicking forward Ben Gronow and full-back Gwyn Thomads, all of Hudderfield, had worn the "Lions" vest. Frank "Bucket" Young, from Cardiff and Leeds, had gone on the first tour of 1910 and so had Bert Jenkins from the same place, while Jim Sullivan had plenty of Welsh support from Risman, W. A. Williams, Ivor Davies, Joe Thompson and Norman Fender in 1932.

The star wingers Rugby League had taken from Wales included Jack Morley, a dentist from Newport and Wigan, and Alan Edwards from Salford; both had their first trip in 1936. Emlyn Jenkins and Billy Watkins, the Salford halves, were from Wales as was centre Gwyn Davies.

The 1954 tour brought the Golden Boy of Wales, Lewis Jones, on to the international scene. Many Leeds followers will say Lew was the greatest Welshman to come north and certainly some of his records will be very hard to beat. His ten goals which I saw him kick in the second Test in Brisbane in 1954 is an example; his 505 points in one season is another.

Benjamin Lewis Jones, who signed for Leeds in 1952, has been the most discussed footballer for years. Hailing from Gorseinon, near Llannelly, he played for Neath and helped Wales win the Triple Crown at the age of 18; he flew out to New Zealand as a replacement for the Lions 1950 R.U. tour and kicked seven goals out of seven attempts in his first game there; in Brisbane he created a R.U. record by scoring 16 points in a Test game, had a second Triple Crown R.U. success with Wales, played on the wing against the Springboks then caused a sensation by accepting a £6,000 fee for signing with Leeds.

He made his debut as a Rugby League player in 1952 and kicked seven goals against Keighley at fullback, but he wasn't long in the game before he had the first of many injuries, a compound fracture of the forearm. He had a "plate" put on the arm but his future was in doubt. He did not play again that season and on his return went into the "A" side. Then the Golden Boy refound his form.

In three matches, against Hull, Wakefield and Castleford, he scored 80 points. Selected as a centre to tour Australia, his 1954 tour record of 278 points was good enough to beat the previous best by Puig Aubert, the French full-back, and Jim Sullivan. Jones's average in Test football was ten points per match. His 1956–7 record of 505 points – 197 goals and 37 tries – was followed by World Cup selection, he had a Cup winners' medal at Wembley, a Yorkshire Cup winners' award and then perhaps his greatest triumph when he captained Leeds to their first-ever Championship success at Bradford against Warrington.

Jones had been car salesman, groundsman and shopkeeper and had not really settled down to a career until he suddenly decided to become a maths teacher. He studied hard and was successful enough to taka a teaching appointment in his adopted city of Leeds, but as his Welsh wife, Maureen, had always wanted to visit Australia the balding, modest genius, who liked the sun too, decided to go in search of it in Australia. He now plays for Sydney Second Division club Wentworthville, whom he has helped win the League Championship. A great player indeed.

Also on the 1954 N.Z. tour with Lewis Jones was a youngster named Billy Boston. a winger who has made quite an impact on the game, Cardiff-born Billy was a star in Wigan's great 1965 Cup Final win and is a firm favourite with T.V. viewers.

The lowest Welsh representation came on the 1958 tour when Tommy Harris, hooker, and St. Helens full back Glyn Moses, stood together with the red dragon, but they never let it be forgotten and were even more vocal than most Taffies. On the 1950 tour, forwards Elwyn Gwyther, Frank Osmond, Doug Phillips and halfback Dick Williams kept Wales to the front in many ways.

The Williams clan have been many. Sid with the ginger hair was groomed to take over from Barney Hudson at Salford but the war stopped his progress. Dick and Evan were two good Leeds half-back signings, while Les Williams played for Hunslet and should have gone on

Lewis Jones, another major signing from Welsh Rugby Union.

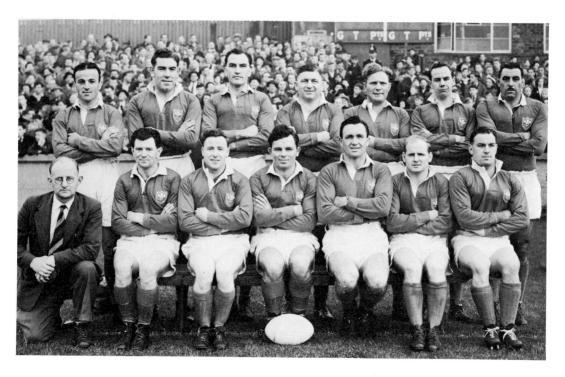

Welsh team picture 1953

tour. The Jones boys have also usually been around the Rugby League world, the latest being Berwyn, who startled athletics when he signed for Wakefield.

The Thomases who have made the grade began with "Dickie", who came from Wales in 1897 to join Oldham. His son, R. L. Thomas, has been a member of the Oldham committee for years, while a grandson, also R.L., was referee in the 1964 Final at Wembley.

Gwyn Thomas, a member of the 1914 and 1920 teams, had service with Wigan and Huddersfield after coming north from Treherbert in 1913, while Johnny Thomas was one of the best halves to come north, joining Wigan and later serving as an official. Two Harold Thomases moved from Welsh Union to League. One, a forward, played for Salford and another was on the wing for Halifax, who had a penchant for Welsh wingers. Apart from Arthur Bassett they had Jim Bevan from Aberavon, both playing in the Halifax Cup success of 1939, and other Welsh wingers who played at Thrum Hall included Terry Cook, Arthur Daniels and Dai Bevan.

French team at Perpignan, January 1970.

The "moderns" from Wales at Halifax include two coloured players, Colin Dixon and Johnny Freeman, while their secretary is Bill Hughes, also a Welshman and possibly the reason why the club know so much about the valleys. One former Welsh Halifax star, Frank Williams, stayed in the town to become sports writer for the *Halifax Courier* for many years.

In post-war football three Price players made their names in Rugby League and were all from Wales: Gareth Price, Leeds and Halifax, took over at Doncaster when the club joined the League in 1951. He was a centre of more than average ability and played for the Welsh team on a number of occasions. He didn't tour with a British team but his namesake, Ray Price, of Warrington and Belle Vue Rangers, did. Ray, a tough little stand-off, played against Dick Williams in the final tour trial in 1954. He gave Dicky a tough time and certainly got himself in to the touring side with that performance. The bashing Williams suffered indicated his ability to take punishment and in consequence both Price and Williams went on tour as the two stand-off halves. The third Price was ex-R.U. centre Malcolm Price, who joined Oldham. Unfortunately, Malcolm received such a severe injury after only nine games that it looked as if he were likely to have a permanent disability; indeed his life was in jeopardy at one point. But he recovered to play again in first-team football.

Possibly more Welsh forwards failed than succeeded. One player who was a great success was Trevor Foster, from Newport. He joined Bradford Northern and became one of the best pack men we have had from Union. He was not only a good player but a good citizen and stayed in Bradford to do useful work for the code, particularly in restoring the fortunes of his former club. Foster coaches at Leeds, where another Welshman, Roy Francis from Brynmawr, was in charge. Francis moved from Wales to Wigan, on to Barrow and Dewsbury and then to Hull. After a successful playing career he coached Hull to a number of finals, including two at Wembley. In the same period Cliff Evans successfully coached Swinton to Championship wins after success as a player at Salford and Leeds. Many Welshmen have made good coaches and Mel Meek, an international hooker, had valuable spells at Huddersfield and Blackpool, while Bryn Goldswain was at Oldham, Hull K.R. and Doncaster. Welshmen abound in this game.

Not all Union players approached by the League sign up. Bleddwyn Williams had £5,000 offered to him to turn professional but refused. Years before his elder brother Gwyn had received £800 to sign for Wigan, money which probably helped Bleddwyn to go to Rydal School in North Wales. Another Williams of the same family did turn to Rugby League when centre-threequarter Keith signed for St. Helens. The "Saints" have had quite an influx of Welshmen of late with big signings like John Mantle, Kel Coslett, John Warlow and Bob Prosser. Two Welshmen were signed on a B.B.C. Sportsview programme, Garfield Owen moving from the valleys to Halifax and Brian Sparks joining Salford.

If I had to name one position in Rugby League where Welsh Union players would have made good consistently

I would have to select stand-off half. There have been many, far too many to write about here. One of the best was killed in the war – Oliver Morris. He was a brilliant player and scored 44 tries in only 61 games at Leeds. Morris signed first for Hunslet, the near rivals of Headingley, and Hunslet officials tell the story that Oliver's father insisted he was given cash rather than a cheque for his signing fee. As a result the Hunslet officials had to stay over the weekend until the banks opened up on the Monday. This wasn't the first occasion it had happened. I once signed a player from Cumberland who demanded his signing fee before he played. He took home a brown paper bag full of sixpences and shillings.

The lure of professional rugby continues to attract Welshmen. The late 1960s and 1970s brought a particularly good crop north, but the arrival of David Watkins at Salford was probably the most spectacular of the era.

Under the guidance of their chairman Mr Brian Snape, Salford had emerged from a dark period in their fortunes and they chased hard for Watkins, the Wales and British Lions stand off from Newport Rugby Union club.

Eventually the persuasive Mr Snape landed his man on 19th October 1967, but it had taken an incredible contract of £11,000 down and £1,000 per annum for five years to tempt him away from the valleys.

It was a brave move by the Salford club and it started to pay dividends from the moment that Watkins made his debut against Oldham at the Willows. The average club attendance of 6,000 was boosted up to 14,000 and Watkins returned part of Salford's investment on the field by scoring a try and two drop goals in their 12 points to 6 win.

Of course it took a while for Watkins to settle into the League game, but he served it with distinction, joining the elite who have international honours with both sides, broke records – he kicked the most goals in one season 221 in 1872–73, captained Wales in the 1975 world series and coached Great Britain on the 1977 World Championship tour of 1977.

He made a brief comeback with Swinton at the age of 37 but retired after a season.

Having scored a major success with Watkins, Mr Snape returned to South Wales in October 1969 for yet another spectacular raid on Welsh Rugby Union. This time his target was Cardiff Rugby Union club's Maurice Richards.

Richards, a Wales and British Lions winger, received £9,000 for turning professional after a glittering Union career that included a record-equalling four tries against England in an international at Cardiff. Still revered in Wales as one of their greatest ever wing creations, Richards has been a success in Rugby League. He was the League's top try scorer in 1975–76, club top try scorer in all but one season from 1970 to 1976 and gained international honours.

Barrow too have never been afraid to dent their bank balance when the right Welshman has become available and in September 1969 they scooped Newport golden boy Keith Jarrett for an impressive £14,000.

The big free-running three-quarter had taken the Union world by storm when he scored an unbelievable 19 points one try, five conversions and two penalties – in one international match against England at Cardiff in 1967 when he was eighteen years old.

His stay in Rugby League, however, was not particularly succesful and his relations with Barrow often stormy. After a brief stop in trial with Wigan he was forced to quit the game after suffering a stroke at the age of twenty-four.

Cardiff was the starting point for the next major raid by League scouts in September 1973. The prize was Welsh international winger John Bevan who was signed by Warrington, an enterprising club who were building a prize-winning side under coach Alex Murphy.

Bevan took to Rugby League like a duck to water and his first season's return of 22 tries helped the Wires win four trophies. Although Bevan is back running a public house in Wales he continues to play for Warrington and figures in British international teams. His famous one-arm-raised victory salute after scoring is famous in the League world.

St Helens have a long, historic connection with Welsh

Welsh team 1947.

Union players. They have backed their judgement on Welsh players many times, but their investment of £20,000 on Llanelli and Wales full–back Clive Griffiths must have taken some nerve.

Their bank manager's face must have turned green when, in only his second game of Rugby League, Griffiths broke his arm. Since turning professional in September 1979 Griffiths has developed into one of the best touch-finding kickers in the game, but he has yet to make his mark on the profssional code. It must be said in fairness to Griffiths, however, that the St Helens team is in a transitional stage and that cannot have helped him settle to his game.

League scouts are always on the look out for potential League talent in Wales. The process never stops. Wakefield Trinity have spent freely during the last few seasons and their back division includes three of their Welsh signings Steve Diamond, Adrian Barwood and Brian Juliff.

Fulham, the London soccer club who entered a Rugby

League team at the start of the 1980–81 season, have been very active in Wales. Their first capture from the Principality was 18-year-old winger Adrian Cambriani, a Welsh youth international from Swansea.

He was the tenth player to be registered by the London club and it was reported that he had signed a contract worth £16,000. He has been so successful at switching codes that he has played for Wales against England in the European Championship.

Cambriani was followed to Craven Cottage by Carl Radbone, a back from Penland Rugby Union club near Swansea, and Cardiff Rugby Union club forward Peter Souto.

A whole host of Welshman are active in Rugby League today. Some come from top Welsh sides, while others are recruited straight from Welsh junior sides.

The risk of failure is still there, as Swinton will readily testify. In 1972 they signed Ray "Chico" Hopkins, an international scrum half, for £8,000 but he failed to make the grade in Rugby League and gradually dropped out of the game.

The trail north, will, I believe, continue to attract Welshman although professional Rugby Union in Wales might just be the thing to stem the flow. Still Welshmen are good for Rugby League and the game is good to them.

# 11
# THE SCOTS

Next to Wales, Scotland has probably provided most Rugby League players from the amateur code, and border-country teams like Hawick, Gala, Melrose, Jedburgh, Kelso and Selkirk have always been a happy hunting ground. Perhaps I shouldn't say "always", for in the early days of Rugby Union there was strong opposition to anyone from the south even watching their games. I was once told how to approach a footballer in Scotland, and the story was born of personal experience. It appears the gentleman in question had gone from Yorkshire to one of the border towns and on arrival at the local station had shown his rail ticket marked from Leeds. He noticed a quizzical look by the ticket collector but never expected the sequel. Walking to the ground he found a body of men waiting for him; word had travelled quickly that a Rugby League scout was in the area. He was approached by the locals, quickly gathered up and taken to the river, where he was threatened with a ducking if ever he came back to that town. Then he was put on the station platform and escorted out on the next train.

But threats and signs saying "No Rugby League men admitted" didn't stop players signing for professional clubs, as the records show. One of the biggest names which helped to break down the barrier was Willie Welsh, an international forward with many caps who joined York and had several successful seasons with them.

Probably the most noted club to take a liking for Scots is Huddersfield, and most of their captures have been good. From Hawick they signed Dave Valentine, who captained the first World Cup squad, toured Australia and later brought his brother Bob to play in the claret and gold jersey. The best centre Scot who never went on tour was Alex Fiddes from the borders. A fine footballer, he gave many years of great service to the Huddersfield club and scored 1,062 points for them. One of his wingers around that time was Jock Anderson, also a border player, whom I once saw run in the Powderhall sprint handicap.

George "Happy" Wilson was another speedy Scots winger. He joined Workington, who made many successful signings from over the border. But it was Whitehaven who obtained the biggest name, scrum-half Brian Shillinglaw from Galashiels. He was later transferred to Wigan for £5,000 but had problems even at Central Park. A good footballer if he could settle in the game, Shillinglaw was selected for a British Commonwealth team to meet New Zealand in 1965 but didn't play.

Leeds had more than one look at Scotland and brought several players back. Among others, they signed Hawick's winger Drew Turnbull and centre Tommy Wright. Turnbull was a success but Wright, mainly through injury, played only seventeen games. As I've often said, "You don't catch fish every time you go fishing."

Leeds bought another Scot, David Rose, from Huddersfield but apart from a World Cup appearance he had a short playing career through injury. The latest pair of Scots to play at Leeds have been winger Ron Cowan and centre Andrew Broatch. If Cowan can stay as long in the game as his brother Stan did at Hull there will be no grumbles at Headingley.

Not as many Scots have been selected for Great Britain as one would have expected. One of the latest signings in the code to receive the honour is Charlie Renilson, of Halifax, chosen for the first Test against New Zealand in 1965. I'm sure there are many more who could do as well if their talent was brought out.

There must be many more in Ireland, too. So far it hasn't proved very fertile at all for League scouts. One of the few who entered the game was John Daly, a former R.U. international, who played for Huddersfield and Featherstone Rovers, with whom he won a Cup Final runners-up medal. But there have been very few indeed.

Workington Town appeared to have made a successful signing from across the Irish Sea when they signed loose forward Ken Goodall fom Irish Rugby Union. He figured largely in their game until injury forced him out.

During the 1960s and the 1970s the supply of Scottish talent moving into Rugby League seemed to dry up. The most successful clubs in tempting Scotsmen were Workington and Whitehaven, but that was to be expected because they are so close to the border. Alex Cassie, Alan Tait and Brian Lauder all served Cumbrian Rugby League well for varying spells.

Wakefield swooped for Hawick Rugby Union Club wing or centre John Hegarty, but a long history of injury during his spell at Belle Vue never allowed him to show his true potential. He was transferred to Dewsbury, but injury continued to dog his career.

Wigan made one of the most outstanding captures from Scotland in League history when they signed George Fairbairn, then a 20-year-old fullback from Kelso Rugby Union club in October 1974.

They paid £8,000 to a young man who was being tipped north of the border as the natural successor to Scotland's famous Union international full-back Andy Irvine.

He was virtually unknown in the north of England but he soon made himself at home in Central Park and in Rugby League where his no-nonsense tackling and brave running were much appreciated by the League-wise Wigan public.

Within twelve months of turning professional he had been selected to play for his adopted country, England, in the ill-fated international championships in Australia and New Zealand, and today he is one of the cornerstones for both England and Great Britain teams.

It was a surprise when he was missed out of the 1979 Great Britain party to tour Australia and New Zealand. He made part of the trip because he went out as a replacement for injured Warrington forward Tommy Martyn, but many people still believe that he should have been in the original squad.

In 1979–80 he took over as player-coach at Wigan,

replacing Welshman Kel Coslett when he departed the Central Park scene. But, despite his gigantic individual efforts, he could not prevent Wigan's first-ever relegation into the Second Division.

His herculean performances, however, were recognised by the rest of Rugby League and he was a popular winner of the Trumann Man of Steel title, Rugby League's highest annual individual merit award.

To bring the Scottish story right up to date, there has been a revival in League club interest north of the border. Spiralling transfer fees within Rugby League have made Union conversions a more attractive proposition again and, during the last few months, there have been frequent reports of League scouting activity in Scotland.

# 12
# THE ENGLISH

The influx of big names from English Rugby Union has not been as many as from Wales. Nowadays quite a number of R.U. players turn professional from clubs in the north long before they become even county players. The League influence in the area obviously has effect.

One of the biggest names was A. B. ("Bev") Risman, who when he signed professional forms to follow in his father's footsteps to the Rugby League code had made a name for himself in Union and played for England on a number of occasions. He signed for Leigh and in January 1966 was transferred to Leeds, where in his first game he kicked three goals. Quite a number of League stars had encouraged their sons to play R.U. first before they turned to R.L. No doubt the financial structure had much to do with this. Ernest Ward, a Great Britain captain, put his son Trevor to the R.U. game before he signed with a R.L. club.

When the break-away came in 1895, a number of Rugby Union internationals automatically went to the League game as their clubs turned to the Northern Union. For example Harry Myers, regarded as one of the best footballers ever to play for Keighley, was capped in 1898 at Union, then played League when Keighley was admitted to membership in 1900. Unfortunately this great player had a sad ending to his career in 1906, when he died after playing for Keighley against Dewsbury at Crown Flatt.

Possibly the first big instance of an English R.U. player turning to Rugby League was the move by E. J. Jackett (Falmouth and Leicester) to Dewsbury after playing 13 times at full-back for England. Jackett's career ended when he had his jaw broken playing against Coventry.

Another full-back from England Union team turned to the thirteen-a-side-game in the mid-twenties. He was J. W. Brough, the Silloth (Cumberland) fisherman who had played against Wales and New Zealand and was then signed by Leeds. The third international full back who was signed into R.L. from an English Union club was Tommy Scourfield, of Torquay, who was actually a Welshman. He was signed by Huddersfield, for whom he played in a Wembley Cup Final. Tom Danby, the Harlequin centre-three-quarter, signed for Salford, toured Australia with the League "Lions" in 1950 and created a try-scoring record on that tour, but Martin Regan who, with twelve Union caps for England, signed for Warrington, wasn't as successful as he had been as an amateur. Union schoolteaching forward Ray French had four Amateur caps in 1961 before signing for St. Helens, where he still plays.

Castleford fans remember with pleasure the deeds of E. H. (Ted) Sadler. He, too, had played for England, getting a cap in 1933 before joining Castleford. In 1935 he gained a Wembley Cup-winner's medal against Huddersfield, who had R. S. Roberts, a former Union star, in their pack. Pat Quinn, a full-back with honours in the R.U. game, had a winner's medal to show for Leeds when he played against Barrow in 1957.

There have also been many players without international honours who entered R.L. from English Union. Devon and Cornwall have been a happy hunting ground for many League clubs and Hull Kingston Rovers signed quite a few players from this part of the rugby world. One of their successes was Graham Paul, signed in 1958 and described as the "Cornish Express". He performed some notable try-scoring feats before retiring and returning to Penzance in 1965. Mike Blackmore, a Barnstaple and Devon winger with many Union honours, was another who moved to Hull.

Clubs had gone south-west in earlier years and brought back good footballers like Fred Rule from Cornwall, who signed for Halifax where he had a successful stay. Winger Mike Wicks from Devon went to Huddersfield and played at Wembley. Ivor Williams, from St. Ives, went to Warrington and the flow has continued from time to time.

Another Union stronghold which produced good League footballers is the Coventry, Northampton and Leicester area, while R. S. Roberts (Huddersfield), Billy Hall and Jack Goodall (Halifax), and Jack Gascoigne were among notable players who "went north" as the Welshmen say. In the Halifax *v* York final of 1931 there were six players called Davies or Davis, four with York and two with Halifax, and if that wasn't enough York also had Harold Thomas and Billy Thomas, Pascoe, Lloyd, Owen and Rosser from the principality.

When the Rugby League Council chairman Mr. A. B. Sharman talked on TV about expansion, he referred to places like the Midlands where he would like to try to start R.L. clubs. He felt a move to London and maybe Cardiff would be the right progressive step. Of course, London in the mid-thirties had two clubs in Streatham and Mitcham and Acton and Willesden, who played in the Northern Rugby League. London Highfield also had a spell of life at London's White City but none of these clubs stayed long, though Streatham bought some very good footballers from New Zealand and Wales and at one point had a position in the "Top Four" in the League.

In recent years the most spectacular signings from English Rugby Union have been made by Salford. They acquired Mike Caulman, an England and British Lion forward and Keith Fielding, an English international winger both from Moseley Rugby Union Club. Caulman switched in 1968, while Fielding arrived at the Willows five years later.

Both proved successful conversions and have joined the ranks of former Union players to achieve international honours in both codes.

Since then Wakefield Trinity have acquired two former Union internationals, scrum half Mike Lampowski and centre Keith Smith. Both signed from Yorkshire area Union clubs and played in the Wakefield Trinity team beaten by Widnes in the 1979 Challenge Cup final at Wembley.

# 13

# TV AND RUGBY LEAGUE

There have been many arguments in Rugby League circles about the involvement of radio and television.

It has always been assumed that the first match seen on television was the Great Britain versus New Zealand Test match at Swinton on November 10th, 1951. Certainly it was the first match televised throughout the country by the BBC. In 1948 the cup final was televised in the London area only. In 1950 the Warrington and Widnes Challenge Cup Final was televised on the Midlands network but a number of viewers in the North-West saw the match with freak reception.

The 1951 Test match between Great Britain and New Zealand from Station Road, Swindon, was a fine baptism for the code, with Great Britain only just winning. There were four commentators, Alan Clarke, Harry Sunderland, Alan Dixon and myself. The producer was Derek Burrell Davis.

In the 1952 season, Workington Town played Featherstone Rovers in the final of the Challenge Cup at Wembley and won by 18 to 10. The whole match was televised. From that point there was considerable discussion and argument about television coverage. One or two clubs refused to be televised and there were many arguments and problems to overcome. Eventually the League accepted the BBC's offer and since many matches were played on Sundays, clubs were willing to allow the cameras in. Wigan, which had been a strong opponent to live coverage, eventually built a special TV camera position in their new stand. Leeds, Castleford, Warrington and Widnes were amongst the clubs which saw the import-

Leeds v Widnes 1977.

ance of providing TV facilities. Leeds, with their under-ground heating plus their own generator, were much in demand during the bad weather period. All clubs in the league have been screened on television, apart from Huyton and Doncaster, at their new ground. Amongst BBC men who had been based in the north and covered Rugby League are Alan Hart, present head of sport in London, Alec Weeks, Bill Taylor, Ray Lakeland and now Nick Hunter and Keith Philips based in the North. A top BBC TV executive is Cliff Morgan who gained all Rugby Union honours possible, and was a much sought after man to turn to Rugby League. He didn't, of course, but he did present the BBC 2 trophy on occasions.

The Rugby League Challenge Cup Final is now shown on television in many countries. Australia, New Zealand

Big Jim Mills gets ready for a tackle.

and America regularly screen the final, with a number of European countries like Belgium, Switzerland and Yugoslavia often showing the big event.

For many years I had advocated Rugby League development in the States. This is now taking place with financial help from some UK officials. In 1965, after the tremendous final between Wigan and Hunslet – regarded incidentally by many as one of the best ever finals – I was flown over to New York to present this 'Battle of the Roses' final on TV. The interest was tremendous and I felt the time was right to make a big effort to get the States really interested in the professional code. At that time soccer had not developed as it has since. Unfortunately there was little follow up of the American Rugby League initiative. Now, with the guiding hand of Mike

Eric Hughes, Widnes escaping a tackle, Wembley 1979.

Mayer, an American entrepreneur and a former football player, the scene has been set for a big effort to get Rugby League established.

The extensive development of the code on television has brought many sponsors to the game and sponsorship money brings in many thousands of pounds. The Wembley Cup Final of 1979 brought gate receipts of around £400,000. A far cry from the gate of £500 at that first Wembley 50 years ago. This year, players on the winning side will probably get £350 each and more with sponsorship. The 'Pioneers' of 1929, the first Cup Final, brought the losers, Dewsbury, £3 a man. Only a few of the players who played fifty years ago in the final were left to meet and to talk and think as guests of the Rugby League at Wembley in 1979 – 50 years on.

Reg Bowden, Widnes
captain, receiving John
Player trophy, 1979.

It may surprise a lot of people to learn that Rugby League, so far as players are concerned, is still a part-time sport. Players are still paid so much for winning and losing and almost all have employment outside the football club and its commitments, which for training purposes amongst many clubs is two nights per week. Now of course there is a heavy match commitment, with many mid-week games.

# 14
# A FEW MEMORIES

## Rugby League Challenge Cup Final 1929
## 50 years on

As a teenager one of my big moments in Rugby League was the occasion when Dewsbury qualified for the first ever Wembley in 1929. On the semi-final day Wigan and St. Helens met in Lancashire and Dewsbury and Castleford in Yorkshire, in fact at Fartown, Huddersfield.

Castleford were almost newcomers to Rugby League, at least at the top level, for they had only been in the league three years, having graduated via the Yorkshire senior competition, a sort of 'A' team football. Dewsbury had surprised even their own fans by beating Warrington at Wilderspool in the third round.

The semi-final would be a much easier job, thought all Dewsbury fans and neutral watchers. The cubs from Castleford had had the guiding hand of Billy Rhodes as trainer, the word coach was not really in existence in those days. Billy Rhodes had played with Dewsbury in his long career but he became attached to Castleford and had many years of experience. His greatest ambition was to take Castleford to the first Wembley. His team trained hard on the small ground where the tea room and the press box were in a tram car near the 25 yards line. The press box was on the top deck.

Both teams relied on home products, unless you call Featherstone, three miles away, foreign, for that was the village where Joe Lyman, the Dewsbury captain and star player, came from. There was an exception in the Dewsbury side in full back, J. Davies, from Ammanford.

"Where on earth was Ammanford", asked Castleford fans and Dewsbury ones for that matter. Otherwise it was an all Yorkshire 'do' and 'Ilkla Moor b'aht 'at' figured amongst tunes which supporters on the main stand and the open side sang with gusto.

The singing dealt with, it was 3 o'clock, and down to the real thing. Lurking on the Dewsbury side, if that is the right word, was a Castleford man wearing a Dewsbury red, amber and black jersey. His name Joe Malkin, a forward Castleford had transferred to Dewsbury for virtually 'nowt'. Castleford fans hadn't rated Malkin, but eighty minutes later they had changed their minds and their tune when 5ft 10 Malkin, rugged, solid and efficient, had played the game of his life. Obviously it was a team effort, with the cheeky Coates Henry of that ilk, who had to sell his Wembley medal some years later, producing his best tricks, but as one Castleford fan said, 'our own man Malkin beat us'. Dewsbury won through in a hard match and Leeds-born, Dewsbury-signed Billy Rhodes had his deepest wish cast aside.

Fifty years on, the enterprising men at League headquarters brought the few remaining players who had trod the Wembley turf for the first time together again. There were only seven left – Henry Coates, Joe Malkin, J. W. Woomore and Jim Rudd from Dewsbury and Johnny Ring, Tommy Beetham and Syd Abram from Wigan. Only seven from twenty six players left, but those not at Wembley were not forgotten. As Henry Coates said, 'we had a marvellous time at Wembley – fifty years on'. A splendid souvenir programme was produced for Wembley. The Yorkshire Post reprinted a good article of fifty years before, as did the Dewsbury District News, although they hadn't thought Wembley was a good idea. Ah well, you can't win them all! David Howes, the League's PRO man, looked back in the special brochure, and Jack Winstanley of Wigan wrote about great 'Sully', the first captain to receive the Challenge Cup at Wembley. In his last playing spell, past 44 years of age, he helped Dewsbury to success.

# 15
# LAST WORD

I hope these few pages of Rugby League history have stirred a few memories and done something toward placing credit for the development of the game in the right place. As one official said, "Those who drink the water should remember those who dug the well." At the same time the proverb that "The mill will not grind with the water that is passed" mustn't be overlooked and there's still plenty of work to be done. One organisation doing much to expand Rugby League is the strong London movement, which is encouraging amateur sides. They have some good ideas for staging the game in and around the Metropolis and although their problems are many I've no doubt they'll succeed. Not least among the difficulties of the new League pioneers is the obtaining of training facilities and I look forward to the day when the R.U. relax their rule prohibiting a League team from using a Union ground. It's rather illogical when R.U. teams play at professional venues, as the South Africans did at Maine Road, Manchester.

Meanwhile, it's a great game and I hope you all continue to enjoy it, whether from your armchair or the stand.

# 16
# RECORDS AND STATISTICS

## CHALLENGE CUP ROLL OF HONOUR

| Year | Winners | | Runners-up | | Venue | Attendance | Receipts |
|------|---------|---|-----------|---|-------|-----------|----------|
| 1897 | Batley | 10 | St Helens | 3 | Leeds | 13,492 | £624 |
| 1898 | Batley | 7 | Bradford N. | 0 | Leeds | 27,941 | £1,586 |
| 1899 | Oldham | 19 | Hunslet | 9 | Manchester | 15,763 | £946 |
| 1900 | Swinton | 16 | Salford | 8 | Manchester | 17,864 | £1,100 |
| 1901 | Batley | 6 | Warrington | 0 | Leeds | 29,563 | £1,644 |
| 1902 | Broughton R. | 25 | Salford | 0 | Rochdale | 15,006 | £846 |
| 1903 | Halifax | 7 | Salford | 0 | Leeds | 32,507 | £1,834 |
| 1904 | Halifax | 8 | Warrington | 3 | Salford | 17,041 | £936 |
| 1905 | Warrington | 6 | Hull K. R. | 0 | Leeds | 19,638 | £1,271 |
| 1906 | Bradford N. | 5 | Salford | 0 | Leeds | 16,000 | £920 |
| 1907 | Warrington | 17 | Oldham | 3 | Broughton | 18,500 | £1,010 |
| 1908 | Hunslet | 14 | Hull | 0 | Huddersfield | 18,000 | £903 |
| 1909 | Wakefield Tr. | 17 | Hull | 0 | Leeds | 30,000 | £1,490 |
| 1910 | Leeds | 7 | Hull | 7 | Huddersfield | 19,413 | £1,102 |
| | Leeds | 26 | Hull | 12 | Huddersfield | 11,608 | £657 |
| 1911 | Broughton R. | 4 | Wigan | 0 | Salford | 8,000 | £376 |
| 1912 | Dewsbury | 8 | Oldham | 5 | Leeds | 15,271 | £853 |
| 1913 | Huddersfield | 9 | Warrington | 5 | Leeds | 22,754 | £1,446 |
| 1914 | Hull | 6 | Wakefield Tr. | 0 | Halifax | 19,000 | £1,035 |
| 1915 | Huddersfield | 37 | St Helens | 3 | Oldham | 8,000 | £472 |
| 1920 | Huddersfield | 21 | Wigan | 10 | Leeds | 14,000 | £1,936 |
| 1921 | Leigh | 13 | Halifax | 0 | Broughton | 25,000 | £2,700 |
| 1922 | Rochdale H. | 10 | Hull | 9 | Leeds | 32,596 | £2,964 |
| 1923 | Leeds | 28 | Hull | 3 | Wakefield | 29,335 | £2,390 |
| 1924 | Wigan | 21 | Oldham | 4 | Rochdale | 41,831 | £3,712 |
| 1925 | Oldham | 16 | Hull K. R. | 3 | Leeds | 28,000 | £2,879 |

| 1926 | Swinton | 9 | Oldham | 3 | Rochdale | 27,000 | £2,551 |
| 1927 | Oldham | 26 | Swinton | 7 | Wigan | 35,000 | £3,170 |
| 1928 | Swinton | 5 | Warrington | 3 | Wigan | 33,909 | £3,158 |
| 1929 | Wigan | 13 | Dewsbury | 2 | Wembley | 41,500 | £5,614 |
| 1930 | Widnes | 10 | St Helens | 3 | Wembley | 36,544 | £3,102 |
| 1931 | Halifax | 22 | York | 8 | Wembley | 40,368 | £3,908 |
| 1932 | Leeds | 11 | Swinton | 8 | Wigan | 29,000 | £2,479 |
| 1933 | Huddersfield | 21 | Warrington | 17 | Wembley | 41,874 | £6,465 |
| 1934 | Hunslet | 11 | Widnes | 5 | Wembley | 41,280 | £6,686 |
| 1935 | Castleford | 11 | Huddersfield | 8 | Wembley | 39,000 | £6,000 |
| 1936 | Leeds | 18 | Warrington | 2 | Wembley | 51,250 | £7,070 |
| 1937 | Widnes | 18 | Keighley | 5 | Wembley | 47,699 | £6,704 |
| 1938 | Salford | 7 | Barrow | 4 | Wembley | 51,243 | £7,174 |
| 1939 | Halifax | 20 | Salford | 3 | Wembley | 55,453 | £7,681 |

Great Britain squad 1978.

| | | | | | | | |
|---|---|---|---|---|---|---|---|
| 1940 | *No competition* | | | | | | |
| 1941 | Leeds | 19 | Halifax | 2 | Bradford | 28,500 | £1,703 |
| 1942 | Leeds | 15 | Halifax | 10 | Bradford | 15,250 | £1,276 |
| 1943 | Dewsbury | 16 | Leeds | 9 | Dewsbury | 10,470 | £823 |
| | Dewsbury | 0 | Leeds | 6 | Leeds | 16,000 | £1,521 |
| | *Dewsbury won on aggregate 16–15* | | | | | | |
| 1944 | Bradford | 0 | Wigan | 3 | Wigan | 22,000 | £1,640 |
| | Bradford | 8 | Wigan | 0 | Bradford | 30,000 | £2,200 |
| | *Bradford won on aggregate 8–3* | | | | | | |
| 1945 | Huddersfield | 7 | Bradford N. | 4 | Huddersfield | 9,041 | £1,184 |
| | Huddersfield | 6 | Bradford N. | 5 | Bradford | 17,500 | £2,050 |
| | *Huddersfield won on aggregate 13–9* | | | | | | |
| 1946 | Wakefield Tr. | 13 | Wigan | 12 | Wembley | 54,370 | £11,993 |
| 1947 | Bradford | 8 | Leeds | 4 | Wembley | 77,605 | £17,483 |
| 1948 | Wigan | 8 | Bradford | 3 | Wembley | 92,500 | £21,160 |
| 1949 | Bradford | 12 | Halifax | 0 | Wembley | 95,000 | £22,000 |
| 1950 | Warrington | 19 | Widnes | 0 | Wembley | 95,000 | £22,000 |
| 1951 | Wigan | 10 | Barrow | 0 | Wembley | 95,000 | £24,728 |
| 1952 | Workington T. | 18 | Featherstone R. | 10 | Wembley | 73,000 | £23,000 |
| 1953 | Huddersfield | 15 | St Helens | 10 | Wembley | 90,000 | £31,000 |
| 1954 | Warrington | 4 | Halifax | 4 | Wembley | 83,000 | £30,000 |
| | Warrington | 8 | Halifax | 4 | Odsal | 102,569 | £18,623 |
| 1955 | Barrow | 21 | Workington T | 12 | Wembley | 67,000 | £27,500 |
| 1956 | St Helens | 13 | Halifax | 2 | Wembley | 80,000 | £29,500 |
| 1957 | Leeds | 9 | Barrow | 7 | Wembley | 77,000 | £32,545 |
| 1958 | Wigan | 13 | Workington T. | 9 | Wembley | 66,000 | £31,030 |
| 1959 | Wigan | 30 | Hull | 13 | Wembley | 80,000 | £33,000 |
| 1960 | Wakefield Tr. | 38 | Hull | 5 | Wembley | 80,000 | £33,000 |
| 1961 | St Helens | 12 | Wigan | 6 | Wembley | 95,000 | £35,353 |
| 1962 | Wakefield Tr. | 12 | Huddersfield | 6 | Wembley | 85,000 | £33,350 |
| 1963 | Wakefield Tr. | 25 | Wigan | 10 | Wembley | 85,000 | £45,000 |
| 1964 | Widnes | 13 | Hull K. R. | 5 | Wembley | 85,000 | £44,500 |
| 1965 | Wigan | 20 | Hunslet | 16 | Wembley | 92,000 | £50,000 |
| 1966 | St Helens | 21 | Wigan | 2 | Wembley | 100,000 | £50,429 |
| 1967 | Featherstone R. | 17 | Barrow | 12 | Wembley | 76,290 | £53,465 |
| 1968 | Leeds | 11 | Wakefield Tr. | 10 | Wembley | 87,100 | £56,171 |
| 1969 | Castleford | 11 | Salford | 6 | Wembley | 97,939 | £58,848 |
| 1970 | Castleford | 7 | Wigan | 2 | Wembley | 100,000 | £93,417 |
| 1971 | Leigh | 24 | Leeds | 7 | Wembley | 85,514 | £84,401 |
| 1972 | St Helens | 16 | Leeds | 13 | Wembley | 89,495 | £86,361 |
| 1973 | Featherstone R. | 33 | Bradford N. | 14 | Wembley | 74,000 | £125,000 |
| 1974 | Warrington | 24 | Featherstone R. | 9 | Wembley | 80,000 | £132,000 |
| 1975 | Widnes | 14 | Warrington | 7 | Wembley | 87,000 | £140,000 |
| 1976 | St Helens | 20 | Widnes | 5 | Wembley | 89,982 | £190,000 |
| 1977 | Leeds | 16 | Widnes | 7 | Wembley | 80,871 | £241,488 |
| 1978 | Leeds | 14 | St Helens | 12 | Wembley | 96,000 | £330,575 |
| 1979 | Widnes | 12 | Wakefield Tr. | 3 | Wembley | 95,872 | £383,157 |
| 1980 | Hull K. R. | 10 | Hull | 5 | Wembley | 95,000 | £448,202 |
| 1981 | Widnes | 18 | Hull K. R. | 9 | Wembley | 92,496 | £591,117 |

# COUNTY CHAMPIONSHIP ROLL OF HONOUR

TITLE SUCCESS
(including joint titles)

Lancashire ...............34
Yorkshire .................23
Cumbria ..................14
Cheshire ....................1

| | | |
|---|---|---|
| 1895–96 ............. Lancashire | 1923–24 ............. Lancashire | 1955–56 ............. Lancashire |
| 1896–97 ............. Lancashire | 1924–25 ............. Lancashire | 1956–57 ............. Lancashire |
| 1897–98 .................Yorkshire | 1925–26 ............. Lancashire | 1957–58 .................Yorkshire |
| 1898–99 .................Yorkshire | 1926–27 ............. Lancashire | 1958–59 .................Yorkshire |
| 1899–1900 ......... Lancashire | 1927–28 ........... Cumberland | 1959–60 ........... Cumberland |
| 1900–01 ............. Lancashire | 1928–29 ............. Lancashire | 1960–61 ............. Lancashire |
| 1901–02 ............... Cheshire | 1929–30 ............. Lancashire | 1961–62 ........... Cumberland |
| 1902–03 ............. Lancashire | 1930–31 .................Yorkshire | 1962–63 .................Yorkshire |
| 1903–04 ............. Lancashire | 1931–32 ............. Lancashire | 1963–64 ........... Cumberland |
| 1904–05 .................Yorkshire | 1932–33 ........... Cumberland | 1964–65 .................Yorkshire |
| Lancashire | 1933–34 ........... Cumberland | 1965–66 ........... Cumberland |
| 1905–06 ........... Cumberland | 1934–35 ........... Cumberland | 1966–67 ........... Cumberland |
| 1906–07 ............. Lancashire | 1935–36 ............. Lancashire | 1967–68 ............. Lancashire |
| 1907–08 ........... Cumberland | 1936–37 ............. Lancashire | 1968–69 .................Yorkshire |
| 1908–09 ............. Lancashire | 1937–38 ............. Lancashire | 1969–70 ............. Lancashire |
| Cumberland | 1938–39 ............. Lancashire | 1970–71 .................Yorkshire |
| 1909–10 .................Yorkshire | 1945–46 ............. Lancashire | 1971–72 .................Yorkshire |
| 1910–11 ............. Lancashire | 1946–47 .................Yorkshire | 1972–73 .................Yorkshire |
| 1911–12 ........... Cumberland | 1947–48 ............. Lancashire | 1973–74 ............. Lancashire |
| 1912–13 .................Yorkshire | 1948–49 ........... Cumberland | 1974–75 ............. Lancashire |
| 1913–14 ............. Undecided | 1949–50 ............. Undecided | 1975–76 .................Yorkshire |
| 1919–20 ............. Undecided | 1950–51 ............. Undecided | 1976–77 .................Yorkshire |
| 1920–21 .................Yorkshire | 1951–52 .................Yorkshire | 1977–78 .................Not held |
| 1921–22 .................Yorkshire | 1952–53 ............. Lancashire | 1978–79 ............. Lancashire |
| Lancashire | 1953–54 .................Yorkshire | 1979–80 ............. Lancashire |
| 1922–23 .................Yorkshire | 1954–55 .................Yorkshire | |

# YORKSHIRE CUP ROLL OF HONOUR
## The competition is now sponsored by Websters

## Webster's Yorkshire Cup

| Season | Winners | | Runners-up | |
|---|---|---|---|---|
| 1905–06 | Hunslet | 13 | Halifax | 3 |
| 1906–07 | Bradford | 8 | Hull KR | 5 |
| 1907–08 | Hunslet | 17 | Halifax | 0 |
| 1908–09 | Halifax | 9 | Hunslet | 5 |
| 1909–10 | Huddersfield | 21 | Batley | 0 |
| 1910–11 | Wakefield Tr. | 8 | Huddersfield | 2 |
| 1911–12 | Huddersfield | 22 | Hull KR | 10 |
| 1912–13 | Batley | 17 | Hull | 3 |
| 1913–14 | Huddersfield | 19 | Bradford N. | 3 |
| 1914–15 | Huddersfield | 31 | Hull | 0 |
| 1915–16 to 1917–18 *Competition suspended* | | | | |
| 1918–19 | Huddersfield | 14 | Dewsbury | 8 |
| 1919–20 | Huddersfield | 24 | Leeds | 5 |
| 1920–21 | Hull KR | 2 | Hull | 0 |
| 1921–22 | Leeds | 11 | Dewsbury | 3 |
| 1922–23 | York | 5 | Batley | 0 |
| 1923–24 | Hull | 10 | Huddersfield | 4 |
| 1924–25 | Wakefield T. | 9 | Batley | 8 |
| 1925–26 | Dewsbury | 2 | Huddersfield | 0 |
| 1926–27 | Huddersfield | 10 | Wakefield Tr. | 3 |
| 1927–28 | Dewsbury | 8 | Hull | 2 |
| 1928–29 | Leeds | 5 | Featherstone R. | 0 |
| 1929–30 | Hull KR | 13 | Hunslet | 7 |
| 1930–31 | Leeds | 10 | Huddersfield | 2 |
| 1931–32 | Huddersfield | 4 | Hunslet | 2 |
| 1932–33 | Leeds | 8 | Wakefield Tr. | 0 |
| 1933–34 | York | 10 | Hull KR | 4 |
| 1934–35 | Leeds | 5 | Wakefield Tr. | 5 |
| (replay) | Leeds | 2 | Wakefield Tr. | 2 |
| (replay) | Leeds | 13 | Wakefield Tr. | 0 |
| 1935–36 | Leeds | 3 | York | 0 |
| 1936–37 | York | 9 | Wakefield Tr. | 2 |
| 1937–38 | Leeds | 14 | Huddersfield | 8 |
| 1938–39 | Huddersfield | 18 | Hull | 10 |
| 1939–40* | Featherstone | 12 | Wakefield T. | 9 |
| 1940–41* | Bradford N. | 15 | Dewsbury | 5 |
| 1941–42* | Bradford N. | 24 | Halifax | 0 |
| 1942–43* | Dewsbury | 7 | Huddersfield | 0 |
| | Dewsbury | 0 | Huddersfield | 2 |
| | *Dewsbury won on aggregate 7–2* | | | |

| | | | | |
|---|---|---|---|---|
| 1943–44* | Bradford N. | 5 | Keighley | 2 |
| | Bradford N. | 5 | Keighley | 5 |
| | *Bradford Northern won on aggregate 10–7* | | | |
| 1944–45* | Halifax | 12 | Hunslet | 3 |
| | Halifax | 2 | Hunslet | 0 |
| | *Halifax won on aggregate 14–3* | | | |
| 1945–46 | Bradford N. | 5 | Wakefield Tr. | 2 |
| 1946–47 | Wakefield Tr. | 10 | Hull | 0 |
| 1947–48 | Wakefield Tr. | 7 | Leeds | 7 |
| (replay) | Wakefield Tr. | 8 | Leeds | 7 |
| 1948–49 | Bradford N. | 18 | Castleford | 9 |
| 1949–50 | Bradford N. | 11 | Huddersfield | 4 |
| 1950–51 | Huddersfield | 16 | Castleford | 3 |
| 1951–52 | Wakefield Tr. | 17 | Keighley | 3 |
| 1952–53 | Huddersfield | 18 | Batley | 8 |
| 1953–54 | Bradford N. | 7 | Hull | 2 |
| 1954–55 | Halifax | 22 | Hull | 14 |
| 1955–56 | Halifax | 10 | Hull | 10 |
| (replay) | Halifax | 7 | Hull | 0 |
| 1956–57 | Wakefield Tr. | 23 | Hunslet | 5 |
| 1957–58 | Huddersfield | 15 | York | 8 |
| 1958–59 | Leeds | 24 | Wakefield Tr. | 20 |
| 1959–60 | Featherstone R. | 15 | Hull | 14 |
| 1960–61 | Wakefield Tr. | 16 | Huddersfield | 10 |
| 1961–62 | Wakefield Tr. | 19 | Leeds | 9 |
| 1962–63 | Hunslet | 12 | Hull KR | 2 |
| 1963–64 | Halifax | 10 | Featherstone R. | 0 |
| 1964–65 | Wakefield Tr. | 18 | Leeds | 2 |
| 1965–66 | Bradford N. | 17 | Hunslet | 8 |
| 1966–67 | Hull KR | 25 | Featherstone R. | 12 |
| 1967–68 | Hull KR | 8 | Hull | 7 |
| 1968–69 | Leeds | 22 | Castleford | 11 |
| 1969–70 | Hull | 12 | Featherstone R. | 9 |
| 1970–71 | Leeds | 23 | Featherstone R. | 7 |
| 1971–72 | Hull KR | 11 | Castleford | 7 |
| 1972–73 | Leeds | 36 | Dewsbury | 9 |
| 1973–74 | Leeds | 7 | Wakefield Tr. | 2 |
| 1974–75 | Hull KR | 16 | Wakefield Tr. | 13 |
| 1975–76 | Leeds | 15 | Hull KR | 11 |
| 1976–77 | Leeds | 16 | Featherstone R. | 12 |
| 1977–78 | Castleford | 17 | Featherstone R. | 7 |
| 1978–79 | Bradford N. | 18 | York | 8 |
| 1979–80 | Leeds | 15 | Halifax | 6 |
| 1980–81 | Leeds | 8 | Hull KR | 7 |

*Emergency Competition

# LANCASHIRE CUP ROLL OF HONOUR
## The competition is now sponsored by Forshaws

## Forshaw's Lancashire Cup

| Season | Winners | | Runners-up | |
|---|---|---|---|---|
| 1905–06 | Wigan | 0 | Leigh | 0 |
| (replay) | Wigan | 8 | Leigh | 0 |
| 1906–07 | Broughton R. | 15 | Warrington | 6 |
| 1907–08 | Oldham | 16 | Broughton R. | 9 |
| 1908–09 | Wigan | 10 | Oldham | 9 |
| 1909–10 | Wigan | 22 | Leigh | 5 |
| 1910–11 | Oldham | 4 | Swinton | 3 |
| 1911–12 | Rochdale H. | 12 | Oldham | 5 |
| 1912–13 | Wigan | 21 | Rochdale H. | 5 |
| 1913–14 | Oldham | 5 | Wigan | 0 |
| 1914–15 | Rochdale H. | 3 | Wigan | 2 |
| 1915–16 to 1917–18 *Competition suspended* | | | | |
| 1918–19 | Rochdale N. | 22 | Oldham | 0 |
| 1919–20 | Oldham | 7 | Rochdale H. | 0 |
| 1920–21 | Broughton R. | 6 | Leigh | 3 |
| 1921–22 | Warrington | 7 | Oldham | 5 |
| 1922–23 | Wigan | 20 | Leigh | 2 |
| 1923–24 | St Helens Recs. | 17 | Swinton | 0 |
| 1924–25 | Oldham | 10 | St Helens Recs. | 0 |
| 1925–26 | Swinton | 15 | Wigan | 11 |
| 1926–27 | St Helens | 10 | St Helens Recs. | 2 |
| 1927–28 | Swinton | 5 | Wigan | 2 |
| 1928–29 | Wigan | 5 | Widnes | 4 |
| 1929–30 | Warrington | 15 | Salford | 2 |
| 1930–31 | St Helens Recs. | 18 | Wigan | 3 |
| 1931–32 | Salford | 10 | Swinton | 8 |
| 1932–33 | Warrington | 10 | St Helens | 9 |
| 1933–34 | Oldham | 12 | St Helens Recs. | 0 |
| 1934–35 | Salford | 21 | Wigan | 12 |
| 1935–36 | Salford | 15 | Wigan | 7 |
| 1936–37 | Salford | 5 | Wigan | 2 |
| 1937–38 | Warrington | 8 | Barrow | 4 |
| 1938–39 | Wigan | 10 | Salford | 7 |
| 1939–40* | Swinton. | 5 | Widnes | 4 |
| | Swinton | 16 | Widnes | 11 |
| | *Swinton won on aggregate 21–15* | | | |
| 1940–41 to 1944–45 *Competition suspended* | | | | |

| | | | | |
|---|---|---|---|---|
| 1945–46 | Widnes | 7 | Wigan | 3 |
| 1946–47 | Wigan | 9 | Belle Vue R. | 3 |
| 1947–48 | Wigan | 10 | Belle Vue. R. | 7 |
| 1948–49 | Wigan | 14 | Warrington | 8 |
| 1949–50 | Wigan | 20 | Leeds | 7 |
| 1950–51 | Wigan | 28 | Warrington | 5 |
| 1951–52 | Wigan | 14 | Leigh | 6 |
| 1952–53 | Leigh | 22 | St Helens | 5 |
| 1953–54 | St Helens | 16 | Wigan | 8 |
| 1954–55 | Barrow | 12 | Oldham | 2 |
| 1955–56 | Leigh | 26 | Widnes | 9 |
| 1956–57 | Oldham | 10 | St Helens | 3 |
| 1957–58 | Oldham | 13 | Wigan | 8 |
| 1958–59 | Oldham | 12 | St Helens | 2 |
| 1959–60 | Warrington | 5 | St Helens | 4 |
| 1960–61 | St Helens | 15 | Swinton | 9 |
| 1961–62 | St Helens | 25 | Swinton | 9 |
| 1962–63 | St Helens | 7 | Swinton | 4 |
| 1963–64 | St Helens | 15 | Leigh | 4 |
| 1964–65 | St Helens | 12 | Swinton | 4 |
| 1965–66 | Warrington | 16 | Rochdale H. | 5 |
| 1966–67 | Wigan | 16 | Oldham | 13 |
| 1967–68 | St Helens | 2 | Warrington | 2 |
| (replay) | St Helens | 13 | Warrington | 10 |
| 1968–69 | St Helens | 30 | Oldham | 2 |
| 1969–70 | Swinton | 11 | Leigh | 2 |
| 1970–71 | Leigh | 7 | St Helens | 4 |
| 1971–72 | Wigan | 15 | Widnes | 8 |
| 1972–73 | Salford | 25 | Swinton | 11 |
| 1973–74 | Wigan | 19 | Salford | 9 |
| 1974–75 | Widnes | 6 | Salford | 2 |
| 1975–76 | Widnes | 16 | Salford | 7 |
| 1976–77 | Widnes | 16 | Workington T. | 11 |
| 1977–78 | Workington T. | 16 | Wigan | 13 |
| 1978–79 | Widnes | 15 | Workington T. | 13 |
| 1979–80 | Widnes | 11 | Workington T. | 0 |
| 1980–81 | Warrington | 26 | Wigan | 10 |

*Emergency Competition

# JOHN PLAYER ROLL OF HONOUR
## John Player Trophy

| Season | Winners | | Runners-up | |
|---|---|---|---|---|
| 1971–72 | Halifax | 22 | Wakefield Tr. | 11 |
| 1972–73 | Leeds | 12 | Salford | 7 |
| 1973–74 | Warrington | 27 | Rochdale H. | 16 |
| 1974–75 | Bradford N. | 3 | Widnes | 2 |
| 1975–76 | Widnes | 19 | Hull | 13 |
| 1976–77 | Castleford | 25 | Blackpool B. | 15 |
| 1977–78 | Warrington | 9 | Widnes | 4 |
| 1978–79 | Widnes | 16 | Warrington | 4 |
| 1979–80 | Bradford N. | 6 | Widnes | 0 |
| 1980–81 | Warrington | 12 | Barrow | 5 |

# SLALOM LAGER PREMIERSHIP ROLL OF HONOUR
## Slalom Lager Premiership

| Season | Winners | | Runners-up | |
|---|---|---|---|---|
| 1975 | Leeds | 26 | St. Helens | 11 |
| 1976 | St. Helens | 15 | Salford | 2 |
| 1977 | St. Helens | 32 | Warrington | 20 |
| 1978 | Bradford N. | 17 | Widnes | 8 |
| 1979 | Leeds | 24 | Bradford N. | 2 |
| 1980 | Widnes | 19 | Bradford N. | 5 |
| 1981 | Hull KR | 11 | Hull | 7 |

# LANCE TODD TROPHY

The Lance Todd Trophy is presented to the Man of the Match in the Rugby League Challenge Cup Final, the decision being reached by a ballot of members of the Rugby League Writers' Association present at the game.

Lance Todd made his name in Britain as a player with Wigan and Dewsbury, and as manager of Salford. His untimely death in a road accident on the return journey from a game at Oldham was commemorated by the introduction of the Lance Todd Trophy.

## The Lance Todd Trophy Roll of Honour

| Year | Winner | Team | Position |
|---|---|---|---|
| 1946 | Billy Stott | Wakefield Trinity (v Wigan) | Centre |
| 1947 | Willie Davies | Bradford Northern (v Leeds) | Halfback |
| 1948 | Frank Whitcombe | Bradford Northern (v Wigan) | Forward |
| 1949 | Ernest Ward | Bradford Northern (v Halifax) | Centre |
| 1950 | Gerry Helme | Warrington (v Widnes) | Halfback |
| 1951 | Ces Mountford | Wigan (v Barrow) | Halfback |
| 1952 | Billy Iveson | Workington Town (v Featherstone Rovers) | Forward |
| 1953 | Peter Ramsden | Huddersfield (v St Helens) | Halfback |
| 1954 | Gerry Helme | Warrington (v Halifax) | Halfback |
| 1955 | Jack Grundy | Barrow (v Workington Town) | Forward |
| 1956 | Alan Prescott | St Helens (v Halifax) | Forward |
| 1957 | Jeff Stevenson | Leeds (v Barrow) | Halfback |
| 1958 | Rees Thomas | Wigan (v Workington Town) | Halfback |
| 1959 | Brian McTigue | Wigan (v Hull) | Forward |
| 1960 | Tommy Harris | Hull (v Wakefield Trinity) | Hooker |
| 1961 | Dick Huddart | St Helens (v Wigan) | Forward |
| 1962 | Neil Fox | Wakfield Trinity (v Huddersfield) | Centre |
| 1963 | Harold Poynton | Wakefield Trinity (v Wigan) | Halfback |
| 1964 | Frank Collier | Widnes (v Hull K.R.) | Forward |
| 1965 | Ray Ashby | Wigan | Fullback |
|  | Brian Gabbitas | Hunslet | Halfback |
| 1966 | Len Killeen | St Helens (v Wigan) | Wing-threequarter |
| 1967 | Carl Dooler | Featherstone Rovers (v Barrow) | Halfback |
| 1968 | Don Fox | Wakefield Trinity (v Leeds) | Forward |
| 1969 | Malcolm Reilly | Castleford (v Salford) | Forward |
| 1970 | Bill Kirkbride | Castleford (v Wigan) | Forward |
| 1971 | Alex Murphy | Leigh (v Leeds) | Halfback |
| 1972 | Kel Coslett | St Helens (v Leeds) | Forward |
| 1973 | Steve Nash | Featherstone Rovers (v Bradford Northern) | Halfback |
| 1974 | Derek Whitehead | Warrington (v Featherstone Rovers) | Fullback |
| 1975 | Ray Dutton | Widnes (v Warrington) | Fullback |
| 1976 | Geoff Pimblett | St Helens (v Widnes) | Fullback |
| 1977 | Steve Pitchford | Leeds (v Widnes) | Forward |
| 1978 | George Nicholls | St Helens (v Leeds) | Forward |
| 1979 | David Topliss | Wakefield Trinity (v Widnes) | Halfback |
| 1980 | Brian Lockwood | Hull K.R. (v Hull) | Forward |
| 1981 | Mick Burke | Widnes (v Hull KR) | Fullback |

# England and Great Britain tours to Australia

| | P | W | L | D | | P | W | L | D |
|---|---|---|---|---|---|---|---|---|---|
| 1910 | 14 | 9 | 4 | 1 | 1950 | 19 | 15 | 4 | 0 |
| 1914 | 12 | 9 | 3 | 0 | 1954 | 22 | 13 | 8 | 1 |
| 1920 | 16 | 12 | 4 | 0 | 1958 | 21 | 19 | 1 | 1 |
| 1924 | 18 | 14 | 4 | 0 | 1962 | 21 | 18 | 3 | 0 |
| 1928 | 16 | 11 | 4 | 1 | 1966 | 30 | 21 | 9 | 0 |
| 1932 | 18 | 15 | 2 | 1 | 1970 | 24 | 22 | 1 | 1 |
| 1936 | 17 | 14 | 3 | 0 | 1974 | 28 | 21 | 7 | 0 |
| 1946 | 20 | 16 | 3 | 1 | 1979 | 18 | 13 | 4 | 1 |

# Australian tours to Great Britain

| | P | W | L | D | | P | W | L | D |
|---|---|---|---|---|---|---|---|---|---|
| 1908 | 46 | 18 | 22 | 6 | 1952 | 27 | 23 | 3 | 1 |
| 1911 | 36 | 29 | 5 | 2 | 1956 | 19 | 10 | 9 | 0 |
| 1921 | 36 | 27 | 9 | 0 | 1959 | 24 | 15 | 9 | 0 |
| 1929 | 35 | 24 | 9 | 2 | 1963 | 22 | 16 | 5 | 1 |
| 1933 | 37 | 27 | 10 | 0 | 1967 | 27 | 16 | 9 | 2 |
| 1937 | 25 | 13 | 11 | 1 | 1973 | 16 | 14 | 2 | 0 |
| 1948 | 27 | 15 | 12 | 0 | 1978 | 16 | 13 | 3 | 0 |

# New Zealand tours to Great Britain

| | P | W | L | D | | P | W | L | D |
|---|---|---|---|---|---|---|---|---|---|
| 1907 | 35 | 19 | 14 | 2 | 1955 | 26 | 13 | 11 | 2 |
| 1926 | 34 | 16 | 18 | 0 | 1961 | 20 | 11 | 9 | 0 |
| 1939 | 2 | 2 | 0 | 0 | 1965 | 23 | 13 | 9 | 1 |
| | (abandoned) | | | | 1971 | 22 | 12 | 10 | 0 |
| 1947 | 27 | 16 | 10 | 1 | 1980 | 14 | 7 | 6 | 1 |
| 1951 | 28 | 18 | 10 | 0 | | | | | |

# INDEX

# Acknowledgements

For invaluable editorial assistance and for the provision of photographs the author and publishers wish to thank John Huxley, David Oxley, Wilfred Slater, Andrew Varley and the Wigan News Service. The author and publishers would also like to thank The Rugby Football League and the British Amateur Rugby League Association for their great help and support during the book's production.

Any mistakes or omissions, of course, remain the responsibility of the author and publishers.